CRITICAL READING

U. S. History and *The Enduring Vision*

Connie A. Cantrell

Rose State College

D. C. Heath and Company
Lexington, Massachusetts Toronto

Address editorial correspondence to:
D. C. Heath and Company
125 Spring Street
Lexington, MA 02173

Published simultaneously in Canada.

Printed in the United States of America.

International Standard Book Number: 0-669-41703-3

10 9 8 7 6 5 4 3 2 1

PREFACE

"Critical thinking" has become the great educational catchphrase of the nineties. The new wave of critical-thinking research relating to instruction and assessment is taking higher education by storm. We are now being bombarded with materials developed to help our students "think critically." Some of these materials are truly useful in our classrooms; many appear to be capitalizing on a new fad and simply apply new labels to old methods in a patchwork way—much like putting bandages on instruction with very little thought to evaluating real needs. Those of us who have followed critical-thinking research and trends during the last few years must be wary of bandwagon approaches to this very real and noble pursuit of enabling our students to think analytically and creatively.

As a college reading professor, I have become acutely aware of my students' needs for productive instruction in reading their college textbooks critically; that is, thinking while reading, using critical-thinking criteria. In my own research, I have found that the most effective means of instruction in critical thinking and critical reading does not lie in isolated exercises covering bits and pieces of "skills." *Rather, students learn best when using content-specific reading materials required in their current courses.* The critical-thinking process comes into play when a student interacts with course content using a questioning process that arises from the inherent structure of the material being studied. Moreover, students become motivated to use the critical-thinking process when they face an immediate need to master the content of a course in which they are currently enrolled. They can see the actual product of their thinking and the added value and rewards that come with using the critical-thinking process. It is difficult and illogical to separate critical thinking and course content as two different areas of study. Students need critical-thinking and -reading processes to acquire a knowledge base in their studies. In turn, a sound knowledge base is necessary if students are to achieve the mastery level of critical analysis required in any college-level course. Thus, students need to build both their knowledge of subject matter and their understanding of how critical thinking is used at the same time; one reinforces the other.

Critical Reading: U.S. History and The Enduring Vision is designed to bring together critical-thinking and critical-reading instruction and college-level course-content material in the study of United States history. Developed as a supplemental guide to be used with *The Enduring Vision* textbook, it aims to introduce students to the critical-thinking process needed for the study of history at the college level.

The guide focuses on these, as well as other, skills:

1. Understanding the bases for thinking historically, including reasons for studying history and methods for exploring and analyzing primary documents and secondary sources.

2. Understanding and using point of view, frame of reference, and author's purpose and tone while reading critically.

3. Understanding and using literal and inferential reading processes to identify the topic, main idea, and related supports within a passage or paragraph.

4. Understanding and using organizational structure and relationship patterns commonly used in history textbooks.

5. Distinguishing between fact and opinion, evaluating informed opinions and conclusions, examining assumptions, and assessing suitability and reliability of sources.

6. Utilizing the critical-thinking and -reading processes as effective tools for notetaking, paraphrasing, summarizing, and concept mapping.

Instructional and practice lessons are built around reading selections taken from *The Enduring Vision*. All practice lessons, or applications, include complete answer keys with discussion and explanation of possible responses.

Acknowledgments:

Critical Reading: U.S. History and The Enduring Vision began as a special project and grew into its current form through the help and support of many talented and patient people. I am grateful to Lauren Johnson, Developmental Editor, for her many hours of work revising and editing the original manuscript; Sylvia Mallory, Editorial Director, for her faith in the project; and Celena Sun, Production Editor, for her part in polishing the final form. I also wish to thank the history faculty of Rose State College for sharing their insights, expertise, and invaluable guidance during the extensive interviews that helped to initiate this project. I am indebted to the many reviewers from across the country who offered ideas, suggestions, and the helpful criticisms that led to development and fine-tuning of the contents. They are Diane Britton, University of Toledo; Jane Fleming, Lewis and Clark Community College; Robert Grant, Framingham State College; Mitchell Hall, Central Michigan University; Jackie McGlade, Monmouth College; Nancy Midgette, Elon College; Al Parker, Riverside Community College; Sally Schwartz, Marquette University; and Stanley Underdal, San Jose State University. Finally, special appreciation goes to Dr. Bill Brown, Dr. Terry Britton, Dr. Phil Cooksey, and Dr. LeTitia Johnston of Rose State College, and to my husband, Jerry Cantrell, for their support and encouragement while this manuscript was in progress.

C.A.C.

CONTENTS

TO THE STUDENT: HOW TO USE THIS BOOK

Critical Reading is designed to accompany the U.S. history textbook *The Enduring Vision* in the belief that anyone taking a college history course will benefit from an introduction to the kind of reading that professors and textbooks require. In history perhaps more than in any other field of study, you'll need to rely on advanced reading processes to understand and analyze the material in your texts.

This guide is divided into three main parts. Each part has a series of discussions and applications intended to help you understand critical thinking and reading techniques. You can use each set in the series separately and in any order you wish; however, you may find it beneficial to use the entire *Critical Reading* guide in its current sequence.

All textbook examples and exercises in the sets are taken from your U.S. history text, *The Enduring Vision*, 3rd ed., by Boyer et al.

At the end of each discussion, you will find suggested responses to the applications in that discussion. After completing each application, be sure to compare your answers with the suggested responses. Many applications call for phrasing answers in your own words, so there are no absolute "right" answers, but compare your responses to ours to see whether the ideas are similar.

I hope that you enjoy using this guide and that you find it helpful in your studies.

C. A. C.

INTRODUCTION

Why Study History?

People study history for a variety of reasons. Perhaps the most obvious is that history gives us a fuller understanding of the present. Tracing events and developments that have led up to the present not only can help you to see the continuities and surprises in history but might even inspire you to speculate about what the future holds in store.

Studying the history of your own country or culture also sharpens your sense of identity. For example, exploring the lives of those who came before you illuminates the connections between values and customs of the past and those of the present. By seeing these links, you may understand better why you live and think the way you do and why you hold certain values.

Finally, studying the history of the different cultures that have come together to make up the broader American culture reveals the differences—and similarities—among all peoples. Learning about differences makes us realize that human beings have developed a rich variety of ways to live, to solve problems, and to ponder the great questions of life. Seeing similarities shows how much more alike we are than we might think. Throughout history, people from all cultures have struggled with many of the same challenges that you face: how to make a living; how to get along with family members, friends, and neighbors; how to live in safety; and how to find meaning in life.

History, then, is so much more than names and dates. It offers a unique richness and excitement that awaits those willing to explore it.

Critical Thinking and Reading

Reading history is a demanding, complex process. You must use advanced critical-thinking skills while analyzing complicated ideas and relationships. Although the concept of "thinking" means different things to different people, the term *critical thinking* refers to a special kind of thinking that entails asking questions and looking for answers as you read and study. Critical thinking demands a disciplined, organized approach to evaluating the ideas that you read, hear, and think about, rather than accepting those ideas unquestioningly.

Critical Questioning

When you think and read critically, you constantly ask questions and anticipate answers. Your success as a critical reader comes from the kinds of questions you ask and your answers to them as you read. Critical readers work to master the art of asking the right questions at the right time for the right reasons.

Whenever you face a problem, conflict, or complicated issue in daily life, your automatic response is to ask questions. For example, if you find out that your state legislature or college board of trustees is considering raising college tuition next semester, your immediate response is to question: Why is this necessary? Are there other alternatives for funding? Can the college absorb decreased funding? What will this decision do to me, my school, my career? As you consider these and other questions, you analyze assumptions, evaluate consequences, and draw tentative conclusions. You acquire information and facts through your questioning, and you continually readjust your thinking and questioning as you work through the problem. Everyone uses questioning tactics to some degree to confront an issue. Your ability to think through a problem is directly related to your skill in asking the right questions and assessing the answers.

Anyone can learn how to ask the right questions. As you practice questioning while reading and listening, you will acquire a "knack" for it. Although you already automatically use this technique every day to some degree, what may seem new here is the idea of applying this skill to novel and difficult tasks. To meet the challenge of studying in college, you must recognize and use your natural abilities to think. Critical thinking represents thinking at its best.

Practicing critical thinking skills while reading will help you to gain control over what you read and how you think about it. If you use the questioning process presented in this guide, you will be able to read, understand, and remember new and difficult textbook material. Moreover, you will sharpen your note-taking skills, participate in class discussions, and answer questions on tests with surprising ease. With critical thinking, history will seem so much more than a mind-numbing array of names and dates. Critical thinking brings history to life.

Critical Reading and Your History Textbook

The best time to practice questioning is while reading your text for meaning. As you work through the applications in this guide, pay close attention to the ones that focus on questioning. Reading well in history requires asking questions that shed light on what the text authors and your instructor are saying about the subject matter. Thus you gear your questions to the text material and to your awareness of the author's intent.

Studying history at the college level is the ultimate challenge to critical thinkers. Without critical thinking and reading, we lose the excitement and lessons that history offers.

PART I

Understanding History

The Enduring Vision tells the dramatic story of the history of the United States, using vivid language and striking photographs, maps, and charts. But the text is more than just a "good read"; it challenges you to understand the broad concepts in historical patterns and to familiarize yourself with connections among key events. To meet this challenge, you'll need to understand the author team's intentions in organizing the text the way they did and the purpose of the text as a whole.

The order of the chapters in *The Enduring Vision* and the ways in which the authors present information are based on commonly accepted principles of historical thinking. The text's structure lets you use your background knowledge to acquire new information and ideas about what you are reading. Part I of *Critical Reading* introduces you to that organization, offers suggestions for building background knowledge, and examines intellectual attitudes that will help you to take advantage of the many benefits that the text has to offer.

DISCUSSION 1: Adjusting Your Thinking

Some students find adjusting to college history textbooks and professors difficult. Thinking back to studying American history in high school, you might see your college history course as shockingly different. Yet understanding the difference between the two kinds of courses can help. In his book *Getting the Most Out of Your U.S. History Course: The History Student's Vade Mecum,* Neil Stout describes one of the most obvious distinctions between American history courses in high school and college. The following selection comes from a section on college course objectives:

These are different from high school, where you got the historical background deemed necessary for good citizenship and in many cases were drilled full of facts in order to raise your Scholastic Aptitude Test scores. A college history course assumes that you have the ability to find out <u>what</u> happened in the past. <u>Why</u> and <u>how</u> it happened, as well as its consequences, require digging deeper. (p. 2)

As this excerpt reveals, college textbook authors and professors focus on the "why" and "how" of history, not the "what." In college, you have the opportunity to perceive history in this new way, to move beyond the facts into the realm of causes and consequences and deeper meanings.

The College View of History

History is more than a simple recounting of the past. It describes human beings' attempts to resolve social conflicts and our efforts to meet the crises that arise when those conflicts are left unresolved or ignored. True history tells the story of real events that happened to real people as they faced the challenges of their times. It reflects the social and cultural trends that came before us and that still influence our lives, our ideas of who we are and what we should be, and our attempts to grapple with the problems that confront us today.

> **NOTE:**   If you have just read the paragraph above without really thinking about what it means to you, try reading it again. It may be tempting to skip over such "theory stuff." Whenever you try to make sense of an explanation like the one presented above, translate the ideas into your own words and try to relate the statement to something familiar to you.

You might translate the paragraph on "The College View of History" into your own words as follows:

History can tell me how people in the past have tried to solve their problems. It can also show me how I and other people living today are influenced by the problem-solving efforts of those who came before us. As I learn about the past, I learn about the present, too.

Now think of an example that demonstrates the concept you have just stated. Base your example on a familiar current issue. For instance, we've seen and heard a great deal about protest movements, past and present. As we study history, we learn that, throughout the past, Americans have engaged in various forms of protest, such as stopping work or picketing during a labor strike, blockading saloons during the temperance drive, and conducting sit-ins during the civil-rights movement. Many times, these activities brought violence and bloodshed. Today, people still engage in similar forms of protest—witness recent episodes of labor strikes and picketing, as well as antiabortionists' blocking of clinics; witness also that violence and bloodshed continue to accompany many of these events. Are there patterns in how Americans engage in protest as a problem-solving device? Have these methods of protest been effective in the past? Are they effective today? What can we learn from past incidents that might help us to work toward peaceful and lasting solutions to today's problems?

Taking a moment to analyze theoretical information will give you an opportunity to go beyond facts and details. By asking yourself why we study history and what history means to you, you will be on your way to thinking critically.

Essentials for Understanding History

As you begin your college history course, it will help to familiarize yourself with certain essential principles of history. Mastering these will let you direct your thinking and questioning as you read your text and attend class. The principles are as follows:

1. All events occur within a social and cultural context.

2. The causes and meanings of events can be interpreted in many ways.

3. Most events have multiple causes.

4. Strings of events form part of a whole.

5. Each event has links to other events.

6. Past and present events are interrelated.

Critical Thinking and Intellectual Attitude

There are three other principles essential for understanding college history. You will need these attitudes, or "mind sets," to think about history and read critically.

First, cultivate an attitude of *intellectual integrity*. When you practice intellectual integrity, you set aside your own preconceived ideas and open your mind to new aspects of familiar concepts. You can then consider interpretations and perspectives that may differ from your own.

The second attitude involves *intellectual flexibility*. When you exercise intellectual flexibility, you accept that there is no one "right" interpretation of historical events. Interpretations of history change in light of new discoveries, and the flexible mind accommodates these changes. Flexible thinking is even more important because it helps you to recognize and analyze the multiple causes of historical problems.

The third essential attitude is *intellectual curiosity*. Intellectual curiosity lets you be receptive to new ways of learning and thinking. Being intellectually curious means wanting or being willing to learn.

Through patience and practice, you can cultivate these intellectual attitudes and use them to master your history course, or any other subject. In fact, thinking and reading critically hold the key to success in all aspects of life.

DISCUSSION 2: Working with Your Textbook: An Overview

Many students find it difficult to know just what they need to do to read a college textbook successfully. You may have learned to depend on reading only for factual information. After all, facts seem easier to remember and give back on tests. Focusing on facts is also consistent with the study skills emphasized in high school. Modern college history textbooks such as *The Enduring Vision* are written differently, and their format does not lend itself well to the fact-only approach.

Trying to memorize only the factual information in a text will leave you lost and frustrated in a college course. Worse, you will understand and remember little of what you have read; lectures, discussions, and tests will seem incomprehensible.

To read and study history as presented in *The Enduring Vision,* you need to understand how and why the text is organized as it is.

Understanding the Purpose of Your College History Textbook

The authors of *The Enduring Vision* have tried to convey broad concepts and principles that have shaped American society. Consider for a moment the concept of integrating the principles of individual liberty within a federal and state system responsible for the welfare and safety of every citizen and the country as a whole. What are your rights as an individual? What are the rights of your state government? What is the responsibility of the federal government? These questions have profoundly shaped the development of American society, as have many other principles that we study in history.

With each passage, or sets of passages, the authors of *The Enduring Vision* encourage you to perceive an overall message, or meaning, underlying the events of certain time periods. They hope that you will understand how one event is connected to other events in the past and how these events provide a foundation for the complex issues that our society faces today.

Historical data and the authors' message are two separate elements, each supporting the other. The authors build their messages on the "why" and "how" of history and on their understanding that history consists of a series of complex relationships. The authors provide details, facts, and descriptions to paint a picture of the social situations surrounding events.

This focus on meaning can make studying the text quite challenging, because it requires a more complex approach to reading than you may be used to. However, it also makes *The Enduring Vision* richer and more engaging than many more traditional accounts.

Understanding Your Textbook's Organizational Pattern

Mastering *The Enduring Vision* will get easier once you recognize the patterns that the authors used in developing the text and you adjust to the reading approach that this kind of textbook requires.

For many years, history textbook writers presented summaries of data, lists of events, names of important people and places, and so on. They put some (usually very little) emphasis on the connections among these things. As a result, the textbooks were dry, and readers struggled to extract meaning from the thousands of facts.

In *The Enduring Vision,* the authors have provided a highly readable narrative description that encourages you to understand not just *what* happened, but *how* and *why* it happened, and what *consequences* came from certain historical events. By using this approach, the authors do not always present information in chronological order. This lack of time sequence may seem confusing, especially if you are used to thinking of history as a series of events to be learned in order.

Time Frameworks and Social Concepts

Each chapter of *The Enduring Vision* covers certain time frameworks. Within these frameworks, the authors trace thematic threads that run throughout our history; for example, the settling of the West and western life, the development of African-American culture, the social and economic issues surrounding slavery and civil rights, the unfolding of the women's rights movement, the flow of immigrants into America, urban development, and industrialization. The authors discuss each of these themes with an emphasis on the social issues they raise. They also try to explain how each issue is connected to other issues, ideas, and events.

To illustrate this approach to history, note how the authors trace the development of African-American culture through every chapter of the text. The text focuses not only on the issues surrounding slavery, civil war, Reconstruction, and the civil-rights movement, but also on the influence of these events on black culture, American culture in general, and current issues in racial relations. We see past and continuing contributions of African-Americans to American culture and the ways in which these form part of the foundation of our society today.

As the text moves on to each social problem, you may become confused about the chronological sequence of events. The focus on issues and ideas can make the text seem to jump back and forth in time. The exercises in Part III of *Critical Reading* are designed to help you to use the textbook as the authors intended. As you learn to work with the textbook's central themes, main ideas, and organizational patterns, you will be able to follow the sequence.

Using a Study Guide

If your professor has assigned the *Study Guide* that accompanies *The Enduring Vision,* use it to focus on what your instructor considers important information and ideas. The *Study Guide* provides an outline of each chapter; lists of names, dates, places, or other types of details that the text covers; and other exercises to help you to review a chapter. You not only need to know the facts but also to learn how they relate to one another. Your instructor may provide additional supplemental material.

Trying to memorize isolated details is time consuming and won't help you to study history in college. To make every hour that you study count, read your text following the methods presented in *Critical Reading.* Use your *Study Guide* while you read, to organize your thinking and to focus on the meaning behind all the facts. Once you have read for meaning, the details will make sense. You will save hours of study time and retain the information you need for exams and class discussion.

DISCUSSION 3: Class Sessions and Your History Professor

All the guidelines discussed in *Critical Reading* for reading and thinking in history apply equally to listening to class lectures, participating in class discussions, and taking class notes. The same processes that enable you to read well will help you to listen and debate well also.

College history professors expect you to study history in an active, analytical manner rather than a passive mode. They want you to see relationships among events and to understand not only what happened in the past but why it happened as it did. During class, you will be asked to focus on this kind of historical analysis. Class lectures and discussions also are designed to illuminate the links between the past and the present. In many instances, your instructor will encourage you and your fellow students to join him or her in *applying* what you have learned from your reading.

Your professor will probably ask you to use your textbook primarily to get the background information that you need to understand class lectures and discussions. Because there is not time in class to cover all the basic information, you will be expected to read the textbook on your own, and your professor will *add to* the information in the textbook.

DISCUSSION 4: Building Background Knowledge

Perhaps one of the most daunting tasks facing college students is that of learning to read for meaning in generally familiar subjects. You already have been exposed to many concepts presented in your college history textbook, but you need to *use* this knowledge from your previous studies and experiences and to *acquire* essential new information. The suggestions below should help you to build your background knowledge.

Recognize what you *don't* know. While reading your text, if you realize that you do not understand an idea, stop and ask yourself whether you lack background knowledge. If the text refers to concepts that you don't recognize, or that you recognize but have forgotten, you may need to acquire more information about the subject.

Turn to the index at the back of your textbook and look for references to other parts of your text that discuss the same subject. Go to the pages listed and see whether the information given there clarifies the topic.

Find another, more basic, history textbook such as that used in a local high school. Call the public school system in your area and ask whether one is available. While reading *The Enduring Vision,* use the more basic textbook to look up explanations of difficult concepts. For example, *The Enduring Vision* presents an in-depth analysis of the effects of industrialization on American life and culture. A textbook designed for a high-school reader will present the same concepts in a more simplified fashion. Do not substitute the simple version; use it as information to help you understand the more complex presentation in your college textbook. Remember that you now need to understand historical issues in greater depth than can be found in a more basic textbook.

Go to a local library or your college library and ask the resource librarian for assistance in finding a suitable general American history reference book. Also, ask about other library resource materials such as encyclopedias, specialized dictionaries, and periodicals. You can use these resources to look up specific references for further explanation. Neil Stout, in *Getting the Most Out of Your U.S. History Course: The History Student's Vade Mecum,* fully describes recommended historical reference materials, among them the *Oxford Companion to American History,* the *Encyclopedia of American History, The Reader's Companion to American History,* and the *Dictionary of American History.* (pp. 21–44)

If your college offers telecourses, look for films that cover the same information presented in your textbooks. These films are usually shown on cable television or kept in the audiovisual department of your college library. Get a schedule of times when you may view the films. They cannot substitute for your textbook reading, but they can serve as an interesting and enjoyable way to strengthen your background knowledge. Many other kinds of films are also available in your college library. Ask your professors to direct you to useful ones.

Develop the habit of using reference materials to add to your background knowledge and to strengthen your understanding of the information covered in your text and class lectures. As your understanding grows, so will your confidence.

DISCUSSION 5: Using Your Textbook as Background

The authors of *The Enduring Vision* know that you need background information and have organized the text accordingly. Each section of each chapter builds on the concepts presented earlier in the text. In each chapter, the authors present an overview of events that unfolded during a certain span of years and discuss a particular social concern that arose during that time. The authors also touch on earlier events that led up to the conditions being discussed.

Understanding this approach is essential for reading for meaning, but it places a very real burden on you. You will understand the textbook only if you know what was presented earlier. For example, it is difficult to comprehend the social problems of the early 1900s if you lack a solid understanding of the industrialization and urban development that transformed the nation in the late 1800s. Remember, if you run into problems when reading a passage that refers to earlier information, turn to the index, find the references, and go back to the pages in the text where you can find detailed explanations.

Learn to use your textbook index to orient your thinking. The few minutes that it takes to reread a section will save time compared to the hours you may spend trying to study something that you do not understand. Be realistic in assessing what you do and do not know. Succeeding chapters in your textbook will build on concepts developed as you read. If you master the content at each step along the way, you'll establish a firm foundation for comprehending new ideas throughout the book.

PART II

Analyzing History

Part II contains examples and applications that demonstrate how historians gather and interpret historical evidence. By doing the applications, you'll learn to "think historically." Thinking historically means asking questions like a historian, putting yourself in the "shoes" of people who have left records from the past, drawing conclusions from what you read, knowing how to separate fact from opinion, identifying an author's purpose and tone, and evaluating the authenticity and reliability of a piece of historical evidence or a historian's account of the past.

To think critically, you need to understand the basics of reasoning and analytic questioning. Part II examines how to apply these elements to the study of history.

DISCUSSION 1: Frames of Reference

Each of us holds a worldview that shapes our interpretation of past and present events and our hopes for the future. We are molded by our past experiences, our interests, our current knowledge, our self-image, our relationships with others, the subjects that we have studied, what we do for a living, and much more. Someone who grows up in dire poverty, for example, probably sees the world differently than the person raised with great wealth. The scientist judges the destruction of the rain forest differently than the farmer in Brazil who wants to cut down trees to farm his land and support his family. A person who has lost his or her job sees conditions in the American economy differently than an economist who assures us that things are improving.

Our worldview provides us with a frame of reference for evaluating historical and current events. Based on our own frames of reference, as individuals we develop points of view toward those events, whether past or present.

Points of View

Educated people are aware of their own frames of reference and assess how these frames shape their thinking and their points of view. They also become aware of—and open to— the idea that other people have different frames of reference and thus different points of view. Educated people acknowledge the differences in points of view and accept that other points of view are possible and worth consideration.

Our personal frames of reference reflect all that we know and have experienced. We perceive events, conditions, problems, and solutions through "lenses" colored by our frames of reference. For example, if you were raised in a home where Christianity was taught, and you believe in its teachings, then the basic tenets of Christianity probably provide you with a frame of reference from which you develop points of view on such issues as the death penalty, family values, charity, and so on. If you also were born in America and grew up influenced by American culture, your frame of reference might include concepts of American democracy and government, along with contrasting concepts of social systems and governments that exist under military dictatorships. These concepts would affect your point of view concerning economics, government intervention in business affairs, individual freedom, education, and much more.

To see others' points of view, we must also try to understand their frames of reference — a difficult task. Often we must attempt to comprehend other points of view while not agreeing with them. It is important to separate the ideas of understanding and agreeing; in order to agree or disagree with an idea intelligently, we must first understand it.

In college, we study science, math, literature, economics, philosophy, history, and other subjects to broaden our frames of reference. These studies expose us to other points of view and give us the tools to evaluate them. When we study economics, we learn to think like an economist. In math, we learn to think mathematically. When we study history, we learn to think historically.

Thinking Historically

To read and study history, you must first consider what it means to *think historically*. You must begin to analyze history from a historian's frame of reference. You also need to understand what historians study, why they study it, and how they go about it.

Historians study social situations, conditions, and problems of the past. They explore the responses of people who lived through those situations and who tried to solve their problems. Historians analyze the past not only in light of what happened and why it happened but in view of how the past has shaped the present and may shape our future.

An important part of the historian's job is to gather as much information as possible about past events, to evaluate the sources of the information, and to analyze that information in a way that reflects what occurred as accurately as possible. The historian then analyzes the events in the context of the social conditions of the times and relates them to other events of significance that happened in the same time period. The ultimate goal of historical study is to relate past events to current issues. How did we get to where we are today? How does our understanding of past successes and mistakes in handling our society's conflicts affect our actions now? From past actions, can we learn what works and what doesn't? Can we prevent conflicts from recurring?

An example of a "current" past event might help you to see history from the historical point of view. Consider the fairly recent Los Angeles riots. If you have discussed the causes of these riots with friends, family, or teachers, you've probably discovered that each of you has a different point of view. The immediate catalyst for the riots may have been the verdict in the Rodney King trial. (Notice that you need background knowledge to understand this reference. Rodney King was not on trial; the policemen who beat him were on trial, and the jury found them not guilty.) However, anyone witnessing the riots, whether firsthand or through TV or newspaper representations, realizes that complex social and cultural forces contributed to the riots and their outcome. These forces have also spurred the ongoing analysis of the social problems that the conflict highlighted.

To understand this event, we need to ask many questions. What occurred during the riots? What social conditions and problems existed at the time and place of the riots? Which of these factors contributed to the riots? What roles did poverty, racial discrimination, and crowded urban living play in igniting the riots? If a politician says that lack of family values in America is the primary cause of the riots, is this true? Why or why not? What made these particular people at this time, in this place, choose violence to respond to their problems? What were the problems at issue? What were the repercussions of the rioters' choice? What is happening now as a result of the riots? How can our understanding of the riots affect the future? How can we avoid further violence? Or can we?

You can see from this list of questions how complex the historian's job can be in analyzing a single event. Fifty years from now, an account of the Los Angeles riots might consist of two or three sentences in a history textbook, if it appears at all. Assuming its inclusion, what techniques might the author use to convey the human drama and tragedy of the riots? Is it possible to analyze the multiple causes and results of such an incident without first giving the reader an overall view of life in Los Angeles in the 1990s? How might the historian summarize the events leading to the riots? How will that scholar's personal point of view color his or her account of the riots' causes, results, and social context? Will one historian's view differ from another's?

As you try to answer these questions, you may realize that historians interpret historical events from a general historical frame of reference, but they also have their own frames of reference and points of view. Read the following excerpt from *The Enduring Vision* to see how your text authors synopsize the Los Angeles riots of 1992:

In late April 1992 an outbreak of civil disorder, arson, looting, and violence erupted in a poor black district of Los Angeles and quickly spread to other parts of the city. The immediate cause was black rage and incredulity (shared by many others) over a jury's acquittal of four white Los Angeles police officers whose brutal beating of a black motorist had been filmed on videotape. For several days the explosion of anger and pent-up frustration raged, leaving some forty persons dead and millions in property damage, and reminding a complacent nation yet again of the desperate conditions in its inner cities. (p. 1063)

Below are accounts of the 1992 Los Angeles riots offered by two other current history textbooks. The first excerpt is from Davidson, *Nation of Nations: A Narrative of the American Republic* (McGraw-Hill). The second account is from Norton et al., *A People and a Nation: A History of the United States* (Houghton Mifflin). Compare these two passages with one another and with the account you have just read from your textbook.

Excerpt 1:

The anger felt in the country had a social edge as well. In 1991 Los Angeles police had unknowingly been videotaped while beating a black motorist arrested for speeding and drunk driving. The tape showed a man, Rodney King, lying prone and being struck more than 50 times by officers wielding nightsticks. The scene gave vivid confirmation to charges that too often racial prejudice led police to harass African-Americans or use excessive force against them. When a suburban white jury acquitted the officers, the black community of central Los Angeles exploded. Stores were looted, some 600 buildings were set ablaze, and more than 50 people were killed. With more than a billion dollars in damage, the California dream seemed to have turned into a nightmare. Clearly, the anger over racism was also fueled by the stresses of high unemployment, urban poverty, and economic decline. (Davidson, p. 1295)

Excerpt 2:

As unemployment and poverty rose, so did racial tensions. In April 1992, when a California jury acquitted four police officers charged with beating Rodney King, an African-American motorist, violence erupted in Los Angeles. In the bloodiest urban riot since the 1960s, forty-four people died and two thousand were injured. Entire blocks of houses and stores went up in flames, leaving $1 billion in charred ruins. According to a California legislative committee, the 1965 Watts riot (see Chapter 32) had sprung from "poverty, segregation, lack of education and employment opportunities, [and] widespread perceptions of police abuse. . . . Little has changed in 1992 Los Angeles." Bush advocated emergency aid, but he passed up an opportunity to address the country's urban and racial problems. "So much for the Los Angeles riots," said a disgusted Jack Kemp, Bush's secretary of housing and urban development. (Norton, et al., p. 1073)

As you compare these three passages, note that each author writes from a somewhat different perspective and incorporates some different information. All three points of view lie within the same historical frame of reference, yet each presents a unique interpretation of the same set of events. To analyze an author's interpretations critically, we need to consider not only that writer's point of view but also the evidence presented to support his or her interpretations. (See Discussion 6 for information on analyzing secondary sources and supporting evidence.)

Historians interpret historical data and strive to support their interpretations with solid evidence. Yet analyzing history is a complicated task. There are seldom "right" answers to the questions that historians ask. Only one thing is sure: historians must be willing to live with a degree of uncertainty about the conclusions that they reach.

DISCUSSION 2: Historical Evidence

The authors of your textbook are all distinguished and well-known historians who have spent their careers finding, studying, and analyzing evidence from the past. Your textbook is the end result of their analyses of this evidence. It provides not only their summaries of historical events but also their conclusions about the significance and interrelationships of those events.

While reading *The Enduring Vision,* try to "tune in" to the authors' historical frame of reference. Join them in thinking historically about our past. To do this, try to think like a historian and to see how a historian uses historical data.

The first step in understanding what it means to think like a historian is to learn how historians find and analyze evidence from the past. The written documents from the past that historians use fall into two broad groups. *Primary documents* compose the first group. These are public documents, records, and firsthand accounts of events by people who experienced or witnessed them. Diary entries, letters, marriage or birth and death records, government records, and official government policy statements are just a few examples of primary documents. The second general group of written documents consists of unofficial documents and accounts or interpretations prepared by others who did not witness the events firsthand. These are called *secondary sources*. Secondary sources usually summarize and analyze primary information. Examples of secondary sources include journal articles and historical writings by recognized historians. Newspaper accounts may be either primary or secondary, depending on the nature of the article. History textbooks such as *The Enduring Vision* are considered secondary sources. Many secondary sources contain primary sources. For instance, *The Enduring Vision* contains hundreds of excerpts and quotations from primary sources sprinkled throughout the text. Your text also presents primary historical documents such as the *Declaration of Independence* in full length in the Appendix.

Primary Documents

To begin thinking historically, you might find it helpful to sample a primary document. Join in a little creative thinking for a few moments. Pretend that you are cleaning out the attic in your great-grandfather's farmhouse. You peer into a dusty old trunk, and there you find a handwritten sheaf of yellowed pages almost disintegrated by time. You begin to read, and you find this:

On the tenth of February, 1675, came the Indians with great numbers upon Lancaster. Their first coming was about sun-rising; hearing the noise of some guns, we looked out; several houses were burning, and the smoke was ascending to heaven. There were five persons taken in one house, the father, and the mother and a sucking child they knocked on the head; the other two they took and carried away alive. There were two others who, being out of their garrison upon some occasion, were set upon; one was knocked on the head, the other escaped. Another there was who running along was shot and wounded and fell down; he begged of them his life, promising them money (as they told me) but they would not hearken to him but knocked him in head and stripped him naked and split open his bowels. Another, seeing many of the Indians about his barn, ventured and went out, but was quickly shot down. There were three others belonging to the same garrison who were killed; the Indians, getting up upon the roof of the barn, had advantage to shoot down upon them over their fortification. Thus these murderous wretches went on, burning and destroying before them.

At length they came and beset our own house, and quickly it was the dolefulest day that ever mine eyes saw. The house stood upon the edge of a hill; some of the Indians got behind the hill, others into the barn, and others behind anything that could shelter them; from all which places they shot against the house, so that the bullets seemed to fly like hail; and quickly they wounded one man among us, then another, and then a third. About two hours (according to my observation, in that amazing time) they had been about the house before they prevailed to fire it (which they did with flax and hemp, which they brought out of the barn, and there being no defense about the house, only two flankers at two opposite corners and one of them not finished) they fired it once and one ventured out and quenched it, but they quickly fired it again, and that took. Now is the dreadful hour come, that I have often heard of (in time of war, as it was the case of others) but now mine eyes see it. Some in our house were fighting for their lives, others wallowing in their blood, the house on fire over our heads, and the bloody heathen ready to knock us on the head if we stirred out. Now might we hear mothers and children crying out for themselves and one another, Lord, What shall we do? Then I took my children (and one of my sisters, hers) to go forth and leave the house; but as soon as we came to the door and appeared, the Indians shot so thick that the bullets rattled against the house, as if one had taken an handful of stones and threw them, so that we were fain to give back. . . . But out we must go, the fire increasing and coming along behind us, roaring, and the Indians gaping before us with their guns, spears, and hatchets to devour us. No sooner were we out of the house, but my brother-in-law (being before wounded, in defending the house, in or near the throat) fell down dead, whereat the Indians scornfully shouted and hallowed and were presently upon him, stripping off his clothes. The bullets flying thick, one went through my side, and the same (as would seem) through the bowels and hand of my dear child in my arms. One of my elder sister's children, named William, had then his leg broken, which, the Indians perceiving, they knocked him on the head. Thus

were we butchered by those merciless heathen, standing amazed, with the blood running down to our heals. . . . the Indians laid hold of us, pulling me one way and the children another, and said, Come, go along with us; I told them they would kill me. They answered, if I were willing to go along with them, they would not hurt me.

Oh, the doleful sight that now was to behold at this house! "Come, behold the works of the Lord, what desolations he has made in the Earth." Of thirty-seven persons who were in this one house, none escaped either present death or a bitter captivity, save only one, who might say as he, Job 1.15, "And I only am escaped alone to tell the news." There were twelve killed, some shot, some stabbed with their spears, some knocked down with their hatchets. When we are in prosperity, oh, the little that we think of such dreadful sights, and to see our dear friends, and relations lie bleeding out their heart-blood upon the ground. There was one who was chopped into the head with a hatchet, and stripped naked, and yet was crawling up and down. It is a solemn sight to see so many Christians lying in their blood, some here, and some there, like a company of sheep torn by wolves, all of them stripped naked by a company of hell-hounds, roaring, singing, ranting and insulting, as if they would have torn our very hearts out; yet the Lord by his almighty power preserved a number of us from death, for there were twenty-four of us taken alive and carried captive. . . .

The story goes on to describe eleven weeks of captivity, during which the writer's small, wounded child dies in her arms. In vivid detail, she describes her physical and emotional anguish. The Indians who have captured her are near starvation and constantly on the move to keep ahead of the British soldiers. She describes her treatment by her Indian captors. They share a portion of their meager food with her. She eats as they eat; she travels as they travel, without rest. They allow her to ride horseback as she carries her dying child. Later, she is permitted to visit her other children when the tribes holding them captive camp close by. She describes meeting the Indian leader, King Philip, and her release for ransom, which is paid by the colonial government. She rejoins her husband, and together they search for and find their son and daughter. Throughout her account of her captivity, she refers to the various tribes that she encountered, their movements, and meetings with King Philip. She describes Indian customs and family life and the Indians' derogatory view of the British soldiers. (*White on Red,* pp. 40–48)

The manuscript is signed *Mrs. Mary Rowlandson* and dated 1682.

Here you are, in the attic, reading this spellbinding manuscript. The first thing you might wonder about is whether the account is true. Was there really a Mrs. Mary Rowlandson whom the Indians captured in Lancaster in 1675? If so, did she really write this manuscript? Did she truly witness these things?

Because your great-grandfather had these papers in his attic, it would be logical to ask him what he knows about them. If he doesn't know or if you wanted to find further information, you would have to do some basic research. Where would you start?

In order to verify that Mrs. Rowlandson was a real person and whether her account describes an actual experience, you could check other primary documents, such as public records. You could research birth certificates, marriage certificates, land and tax records, government records concerning Indian captives and ransoms, and so on. You could also check secondary documents, such as histories of the New England Indian wars in the late 1600s (in this case, "King Philip's War" in the colonies) to find out more about Indian raids and captives at that time.

Once you ask these questions and start trying to find the answers, you are thinking like a historian.

The excerpt above was taken from *A Narrative of the Captivity and Restoration of Mrs. Mary Rowlandson,* 1682. During the conflict in New England known as King Philip's War, Mrs. Rowlandson, the wife of the minister of Lancaster, was taken captive by Indians in 1675 and held for eleven weeks. After she was ransomed and returned to her husband, she wrote a vivid description of her captivity. The manuscript was written as a kind of journal, and, according to her, was published at the request of friends. The full document is too long to be shown here, and these excerpts provide only a glimpse of her writing. Indeed, it is difficult to do justice to a primary document without showing it in its entirety. If you would like to read the full account, you can find it in Lauter et al., *The Heath Anthology of American Literature* (D. C. Heath and Co.)

Clearly, a firsthand account like this one gives us dramatic insight into the past. There are many such accounts written by former captives of Indians in the 1600s and 1700s. Their descriptions of life among the Native Americans as seen through the eyes of a captive offer historians a wealth of information. From these accounts, we learn not only about the suffering of the captives, but also about the general plight and suffering of their captors. We learn much about the Indian societies in which the captives lived. In cases in which captives were accepted by Indian societies, we get a rare glimpse into Native American life and culture.

DISCUSSION 3: Analyzing Primary Documents*

If you were a historian discovering the Rowlandson manuscript, the first thing you would do would be to *verify the source.* You would ask:

1. Who is the author? What other information do I have about the author that will help me to determine whether he or she is a reliable witness?

2. Was the author in a position to have witnessed the events as he or she claims? What information do I have to confirm that the author really observed the events described?

3. Does the description of events seem accurate?

As we saw from the Indian-captive example in Discussion 2, you can find the answers to these questions through basic research. Yet you can imagine how much time and meticulous care such verification requires. Nevertheless, primary accounts by eyewitnesses have to be researched this way in order for historians to trust their authenticity.

Analyzing Frame of Reference and Point of View

Primary documents can paint a powerful picture. They also reflect a single point of view. A captive of the Indians will provide only one perspective of the experience. No doubt, an eyewitness account by an Indian who saw the same events would be told differently. Not surprisingly, there are very few firsthand accounts of King Philip's War available that are written by Indians. Indeed, it is often said that those who win the war write the history. In the case of the Indian wars in the early years of white settlement, much Indian culture was destroyed or disregarded. Consequently, most surviving historical accounts come from the white American or European perspective.

Frame of Reference

To analyze *any* written account, we need to evaluate the author's frame of reference. You can determine the frame of reference by analyzing the document itself and by assessing background information about the author.
A historian would ask:

1. What is the author's frame of reference? What do we know about the author's background that would help us to determine his or her frame of reference?

2. What evidence in the manuscript would help us to understand this author's worldview?

APPLICATION 3A: Look again at the excerpt from Mary Rowlandson's manuscript. Then answer the following questions:

1. What is Mrs. Rowlandson's frame of reference?

---

*For this section, refer to the Mary Rowlandson account shown in the previous discussion.

2. What experiences and background appear to have shaped how she sees the events that she describes?

Compare your responses with those shown at the end of Discussion 3.

Point of View

As you practice thinking historically, try to determine the author's point of view in every primary document. An author's point of view "grows" directly from his or her frame of reference. If you were to read the entire Rowlandson manuscript, you would see a number of places where Mrs. Rowlandson expresses a point of view. Based on the short passage that you have read, you should be able to analyze Mrs. Rowlandson's point of view regarding the Indians. Ask yourself:

1. Does the written account reflect the author's point of view?

2. In what ways is that point of view expressed?

APPLICATION 3B: Answer the questions below concerning Rowlandson's account of her capture; then compare your response with the suggested responses at the end of Discussion 3.

1. Does Mrs. Rowlandson's account reflect a point of view?

2. If so, in what ways is her point of view expressed?

Determining Fact and Opinion

Analyzing documents for fact and opinion gets at the very heart of evaluating historical evidence. To distinguish fact from opinion, the historian asks:

1. What events and circumstances described by the author might be considered factual? (In other words, what elements of the account can be verified by other sources?) Statements of fact generally can be evaluated as true or false through comparing the statements with other records and eyewitness accounts. Statements of fact also can be confirmed or denied by all who witnessed the event.

2. What statements by the author might be considered opinion? (What elements of the account are based on the interpretations, judgments, and evaluations of the author and are not possible to verify?)

Now we come to the tough part, that is, evaluating the article's veracity and separating fact and opinion. Think of determining fact and opinion as the process that juries use during a trial as they listen to testimony. If you had to serve on the jury for a murder trial, what questions would you ask in your own mind as the witnesses testified?

APPLICATION 3C: Look once more at the Rowlandson passage, and ask yourself the following questions. Compare your answers to the suggested responses.

1. Which elements of Mrs. Rowlandson's account could be considered fact?

2. Which elements of her account appear to be opinion?

A good example of a statement of opinion is the section in which Rowlandson says, "It is a solemn sight to see so many Christians lying in their blood, some here, and some there, like a company of sheep torn by wolves, all of them stripped naked by a company of hell-hounds, roaring, singing, ranting and insulting, as if they would have torn our very hearts out; yet the Lord by his almighty power preserved a number of us."

> **NOTE:** In other sections of the Rowlandson account (not shown in the excerpt printed in Discussion 2), we also learn much about the Indian captors' *lack* of savagery by "reading between the lines." For example, as Rowlandson describes the heartbreak of carrying her dying child while being forced to flee with the attackers, she tells of being allowed to ride horseback while many of the Indians traveled on foot. She was fed a portion of the same food her captors ate even though there was not enough to sustain the strength of the tribe. She was allowed to go unsupervised to visit her children who were held captive in other camps. Even so, she describes these events in the same manner as that shown in the excerpt you have read—from the perspective of a victim of "savages."

SUGGESTED RESPONSES to Discussion 3:

> **NOTE:** The suggested-response sections throughout this guide are provided to help you check *your understanding of the questioning process* used in the applications. The responses are suggestions only and are not intended to be used as "right" answers. In fact, your responses will probably be worded differently from these. Use the suggested responses mainly to compare overall ideas.

Application 3A:

1. *What is Mrs. Rowlandson's frame of reference?* Mrs. Rowlandson's frame of reference is that of a white woman living in a frontier settlement in New England in the mid-to-late 1600s. A mother of three, she views the world as a mature woman concerned about her children and family.

2. *What experiences and background appear to have shaped how she sees the events that she describes?* Her many references to the Bible and her word choice suggest that she is religious, probably a Puritan, certainly a Christian.

Application 3B:

1. *Does Mrs. Rowlandson's account reflect the author's point of view?* Mrs. Rowlandson considers the Indians who captured her to be totally savage. Her vivid descriptions of the raid on her home are told from the point of view of a victim of the horrifying ordeal.

2. *If so, in what ways is her point of view expressed?* Her point of view concerning the Indians is expressed by such words as *savages, heathens, barbarous,* and so on, and by the manner in which she describes the attackers' brutality. Also consider the many ways in which Mrs. Rowlandson indicates her religious frame of reference. How does she view the events in terms of Divine Will?

Application 3C:

1. *What elements of Mrs. Rowlandson's account could be considered fact?* Elements of the account that could be verified would be that Indians did raid Lancaster in 1675 and did take captives and kill settlers. It would be difficult to verify the manner in which the settlers were captured and/or killed unless we had other eyewitness accounts of the same event. Mary Rowlandson states the manner in which several died or were captured as statements of fact, and we assume that if other accounts existed, Rowlandson's statements could be found to be true or false. The number of dead and captured could be verified and are accepted as statements of fact.

2. *What elements of her account appear to be opinion?* Point of view and statements of opinion are closely related. Mary Rowlandson's statements are somewhat mixed in fact and opinion. Her opinion emerges in such descriptive phrases as "murderous wretches," "bloody heathen," and "the Indians scornfully shouted." She offers her eyewitness account in descriptive terms that reflect her opinion. In some sections, she offers statements of opinion as she tells her thoughts and her feelings about the event.

DISCUSSION 4: Comparing Primary Documents

Now that you have sampled a primary document describing the savagery of the Indians from a white Indian captive's perspective, it might be interesting to read another account that will make you wonder who was the "savage."

The following account was written by William Bradford, governor of Plymouth. In it, he describes the destruction of the New England Pequot Indians by the British military in 1636, many years before the Lancaster raid. The British surrounded the main Pequot village and set it on fire, nearly exterminating the Pequots. Governor Bradford writes this description:

And those that first entered found sharp resistance from the enemy who both shot at and grappled with them; others ran into their houses and brought out fire and set them on fire, which soon took in their mat; and standing close together, with the wind all was quickly on a flame, and thereby more were burnt to death than was otherwise slain; It burnt their bowstrings and made them unserviceable; those that scaped the fire were slain with the sword, some hewed to pieces, others run through with their rapiers, so as they were quickly dispatched and very few escaped. It was conceived they thus destroyed about 400 at this time. It was a fearful sight to see them thus frying in the fire and the streams of blood quenching the same, and horrible was the stink and scent thereof; but the victory seemed a sweet sacrifice, and they gave the praise thereof to God, who had wrought so wonderfully for them, thus to enclose their enemies in their hands and give them so speedy a victory over so proud and insulting an enemy. (p. 55)

APPLICATION 4A: Ask yourself the following questions about frame of reference, point of view, and fact and opinion for this document. Compare your answers with the suggested responses that follow Discussion 4.

1. What is the author's frame of reference?

2. Does the written account reflect the author's point of view?

3. In what ways is that point of view expressed?

4. Which elements of the account could be considered fact?

5. Which elements of the account appear to be opinion?

APPLICATION 4B: Now consider the following example of another primary document. As you read, ask yourself the critical questions used in Application 4A. Compare your responses with our suggested responses.

The account below was written by John Lawson, an English-born gentleman-surveyor who came to North Carolina in 1701 and made several expeditions into Indian country. Lawson described the Indians whom he met in the early 1700s. In his *History of North Carolina*, published in England in 1709, he wrote the following:

Excerpt 1:

They are very kind and charitable to one another, but more especially to those of their own Nation; (here he describes in detail how they help anyone in their tribe who is in need). They have no Fence to part one anothers Lots in their Corn-Field, but every Man knows his own, and it scarce ever happens that they rob one another of so much as an Ear of Corn, which, if any is found to do, he is sentenced by the Elders to work and plant for him that was robbed, till he is recompensed for all the Damage he has suffered in his Corn-Field; and this is punctually performed, and the Thief held in Disgrace that steals from any of his Country-Folks. It often happens that a Woman is destitute of her Husband, and has a great many Children to maintain; such a Person they always help, and make their young men plant, reap, and do every thing that she is not capable of doing herself; yet they do not allow any one to be idle, but to employ themselves in some Work or other.

Excerpt 2:

There is one Vice very common everywhere, which I never found amongst them, which is, Envying other Men's happiness, because their station is not equal to, or above their Neighbors. Of this Sin I cannot say I ever saw an Example, though they are a People that set as great a Value upon themselves, as any sort of Men, in the World, upon which Account they find something Valuable in themselves above Riches. (Vogil 43–44)

NOTE: It is interesting to compare and contrast the frames of reference, points of view, and fact and opinion that influence the Rowlandson, Bradford, and Lawson accounts. Take a moment to consider the similarities and differences in frame of reference and point of view. Ask yourself why different frames of reference elicit different points of view. This type of analysis is a fundamental part of thinking and reading critically.

Historians view and compare large numbers of primary documents. With each document, they ask the questions listed in Discussions 3 and 4. They then try to detect fact and bias in the accounts. After analyzing many documents, historians find certain patterns emerging that give clues as to what actually happened and why. As they assemble and compare documents, they search for an overall view, not only of the sequence of events, but also of the possible causes and effects of the events, as well as surrounding circumstances.

SUGGESTED RESPONSES to Discussion 4:

Application 4A:

1. *What is the author's frame of reference?* Governor Bradford's frame of reference is that of a government official reporting details of a military engagement. A prominent leader in the New England colonies, he represents a white European Christian perspective.

2. *Does the written account reflect the author's point of view?* Governor Bradford's point of view is indeed reflected in this account. He describes the military encounter in detail as official documentation. He is obviously pleased with the outcome of the battle and credits God with the victory over the enemy.

3. *In what ways is that point of view expressed?* The first part of the account contains a factual, though descriptive, view of the military engagement that indicates a military or governmental point of view. The point of view of a "victor" is expressed in the wording used in the last few lines of the excerpt: "victory seemed a sweet sacrifice." The statement "They gave praise thereof to God, who had wrought so wonderfully for them" reveals the writer's religious orientation.

4. *Which elements of the account could be considered fact?* The details of the battle could be verified by other eyewitness accounts and could therefore be considered statements of fact.

5. *Which elements of the account appear to be opinion?* Statements indicating opinion begin with the line, "It was a fearful sight to see them thus frying in the fire and the streams of blood quenching the same. . . ." The remainder of the account appears to express opinion throughout. A good example of a statement of opinion is the last sentence, which uses such wording as "so proud and insulting an enemy."

Application 4B:

1. *What is the author's frame of reference?* Lawson's frame of reference is that of a white European traveling freely among the Indians. His presence is apparently accepted by the tribes about whom he is writing. His frame of reference also appears to be somewhat academic or professional as he attempts to describe Indian culture.

2. *Does the account reflect the author's point of view?* In point of view, Lawson seems open to accepting and valuing Indian culture. He clearly admires the virtues he describes.

3. *In what ways is point of view expressed?* Wording throughout the excerpts reflects Lawson's point of view. He describes the Indians as "kind and charitable to one another." Positive words are used to describe how they help one another. The second paragraph presents a highly positive point of view concerning his perception of their self-esteem and apparent lack of envy.

4. *Which elements of the account could be considered fact?* In the first paragraph, Lawson describes observable cultural mores such as the punishment for stealing and the protection of widows. These are presented as statements of fact.

5. *Which elements of the account appear to be opinion?* In the second paragraph, Lawson offers statements of opinion as he interprets and evaluates what he deems a virtue—the Indians' lack of envy. His choice of wording is highly positive and complimentary.

DISCUSSION 5: Contrasting Documents

One way to understand the historical thinking essential for evaluating documents is to read contrasting primary documents about the same event. Each author's frame of reference and point of view will influence the choice of details presented and will shape the author's opinions. Statements of fact and opinion also have direct links to the author's purpose and tone. Historians analyze the documents by asking questions about the author's intentions and the manner in which he or she presents statements.

Purpose and Tone

All historical documents must be analyzed for purpose and tone. The historian asks questions about the author's motives for offering an account in a certain way. An author's purpose, for example, might be to inform, to describe, to persuade, or to entertain. Tone refers to the manner in which the author presents the account. We can assess tone by observing how the account is worded. In the Rowlandson account, the author's purpose appears to be narrative description. Her choice of wording sets a tone of fear, dread, and despair. An analysis of Governor Bradford's account (Discussion 4) reveals that the author wants mainly to inform and describe. His word choice creates a tone of pride in the destruction of the enemy. We detect relatively little sympathy for the victims of the battle that he describes. Lawson's intent seems to be that of describing and probably informing. His tone indicates admiration for the Indians whom he observes.

Application 5 below provides an excellent opportunity to detect and analyze purpose and tone in contrasting documents and illustrates the important role that these two aspects play in the authors' messages.

APPLICATION 5:   The following excerpts come from *Facts on File*, Feb. 28, 1992, pp. 134–135. The excerpts in Set 1 describe the start of active fighting in the Gulf War of 1991; Set 2 concerns the end of the active ground fighting as Iraq withdrew from Kuwait. Each set has two excerpts: one from a speech by George Bush, and one (shaded) from a speech by Saddam Hussein. As you read the selections, ask yourself questions about the frame of reference, point of view, fact and opinion, and purpose and tone in each account.

Set 1:

4. Bush Announces Ground Offensive

Text of President Bush's televised address Feb. 23 at 10:00 a.m. announcing the launching of a ground offensive against Iraqi forces:

Yesterday, after conferring with my senior national security advisers and following extensive consultations with our coalition partners, Saddam Hussein was given one last chance, set forth in very explicit terms, to do what he should have done more than six months ago: withdraw from Kuwait without condition or further delay and comply fully with the resolutions passed by the United Nations Security Council.

Regrettably, the noon deadline passed without the agreement of the government of Iraq to meet demands of United Nations Security Council Resolution 660, as set forth in the specific terms spelled out by the coalition to withdraw unconditionally from Kuwait.

To the contrary, what we have seen is a redoubling of Saddam Hussein's efforts to destroy completely Kuwait and its people.

I have therefore directed [allied commander] Gen. Norman Schwarzkopf, in conjunction with coalition forces, to use all forces available, including ground forces, to eject the Iraqi army from Kuwait.

Once again, this was a decision made only after extensive consultations within our coalition partnership. The liberation of Kuwait has now entered a final phase. I have complete confidence in the ability of the coalition forces swiftly and decisively to accomplish their mission.

Tonight as this coalition of countries seeks to do that which is right and

5. Hussein Urges Troops to Fight

The following are excerpts from a Feb. 24 speech by Iraqi President Saddam Hussein over Baghdad radio in response to the allied attack:

O great Iraqi people, O valiant men of our heroic armed forces. O faithful and honorable people wherever you are . . . at the time when it was decided that the [U.N.] Security Council would meet to look into the Soviet peace initiative, which we supported . . . the treacherous Bush and his filthy agent [Saudi Arabian King] Fahd, and others who have consorted with them in committing crimes, shame and aggression, committed the treachery.

Those cowards who have perfected the acts of treachery, treason and vileness, committed treachery after they departed from every path of virtue, goodness and humanity. They have committed treachery and waged their large-scale ground assault against our struggling forces this morning. Their objective became known to all who have not known their objective so far. . . .

They betrayed everyone but God is above all . . . He will strike back their treachery on their necks and shame them until their ranks and their failing horde are repulsed. . . .

Fight them, O Iraqis, with all the values that you imbibed from your great history and with all the values of faith in which you believed as a people who believe in God . . . fight them, O brave, splendid men.

Fight them because with their defeat you will be at the last entrance of the conquest of all conquests. The war will just, I ask only that all of you stop what you were doing and say a prayer for all the coalition forces, and especially for our men and women in uniform, who this very moment are risking their lives for their country and for all of us.

May God bless and protect each and every one of them and may God bless the United States of America.

Thank you very much.

end with all that the situation entails of dignity, glory and triumph for your people, army and nation.

If the opposite takes place, God forbid, there will only be the deep abyss to which the enemies are aspiring to push you . . . and a lengthy darkness will prevail over Iraq.

Fight them and show no mercy toward them, for this is how God wishes the faithful to fight the infidel. Your sons, mothers, fathers and kin, and the entire population of Iraq and the world are beholding your performance today. Do what pleases God and bring dignity to the homeland and the people. . . .

Victory is sweet with the help of God.

Set 2:

8. Hussein Affirms Withdrawal, Claims Victory

The following are excerpts of a speech by Saddam Hussein, broadcast over Baghdad radio early Feb. 26, in which he personally announced the Iraqi withdrawal but claimed victory for his cause:

. . . . The harvest in the mother of battles has succeeded. After we have harvested what we have harvested, the greater harvest and its yield will be in the time to come, and it will be much greater than what we have at present, in spite of what we have at present in terms of victory, dignity and glory that was based on the sacrifices of a deep faith which is generous without any hesitation or fear. . . .

O valiant Iraqi men, O glorious Iraqi women, Kuwait is part of our country and was carved from it in the past. Circumstances today have willed that it remain in the state in which it will

10. Bush Declares Victory Over Iraq

Following is the text of President Bush's televised address from the Oval Office Feb. 27 declaring a successful conclusion to the ground war:

Kuwait is liberated. Iraq's army is defeated. Our military objectives are met. Kuwait is once more in the hands of Kuwaitis in control of their own destiny. We share in their joy, a joy tempered only by our compassion for their ordeal.

Tonight, the Kuwaiti flag once again flies above the capital of a free and sovereign nation, and the American flag flies above our embassy.

Seven months ago, America and the world drew a line in the sand. We declared that the aggression against Kuwait would not stand, and tonight America and the world have kept their word. This is not a time to gloat, but it is a time of pride, pride in our troops, remain after the withdrawal of our struggling forces from it. It hurts you that this should happen.

We rejoiced on the day of the call when it was decided that Kuwait should be one of the main gates for deterring the plot and for defending all Iraq from the plotters. We say that we will remember Kuwait on the great day of the call, on the days that followed it, and in documents and events, some of which date back 70 years.

The Iraqis will remember and will not forget that on 8 August, 1990, Kuwait became part of Iraq legally, constitutionally and actually. They remember and will not forget that it remained throughout this period from 8 August 1990 and until last night, when withdrawal began, and today we will complete withdrawal of our forces, God willing.

Today, certain circumstances made the Iraqi Army withdraw as a result of the ramifications which we mentioned, including the combined aggression by 30 countries. Their repugnant siege has been led in evil and aggression by the machine and the criminal entity of America and its major allies. . . .

Everyone will remember that the gates of Constantinople were not opened before the Moslems in the first struggling attempt. . . . By virtue of the struggle of the Palestinians and Iraqis, Palestine has returned anew to knock at the doors closed on evil. . . .

Shout for victory, O brothers; shout for your victory and the victory of all honorable people. O Iraqis. You have fought 30 countries, and all the evil and the largest machine of war and destruction in the world that surrounds them.

The soldiers of faith have triumphed over the soldiers of wrong, O stalwart men. Your God is the one who granted your victory. You triumphed when you rejected, in the name of

pride in the friends who stood with us in the crisis, pride in our nation and the people whose strength and resolve made victory quick, decisive and just.

And soon we will open wide our arms to welcome back home to America our magnificent fighting forces. No one country can claim this victory as its own. It was not only a victory for Kuwait, but a victory for all the coalition partners. This is a victory for the United Nations, for all mankind, for the rule of law and for what is right.

After consulting with Secretary of Defense [Richard] Cheney, the Chairman of the Joint Chiefs of Staff, Gen. [Colin] Powell, and our coalition partners, I am pleased to announce that at midnight tonight, Eastern Standard Time, exactly 100 hours since ground operations commenced and six weeks since the start of Operation Desert Storm, all United States and coalition forces will suspend offensive combat operations.

It is up to Iraq whether this suspension on the part of the coalition becomes a permanent cease-fire. Coalition, political and military terms for a formal cease-fire include the following requirements:

- Iraq must release immediately all coalition prisoners of war, third-country nationals and the remains of all who have fallen.
- Iraq must release all Kuwaiti detainees.
- Iraq also must inform Kuwaiti authorities of the location and nature of all land and sea mines.
- Iraq must comply fully with all relevant United Nations Security Council resolutions. This includes a rescinding of Iraq's August decision to annex Kuwait and acceptance in principle of Iraq's responsibility to pay compensation for the loss, damage and injury its aggression has caused.

faith, the will of evil which the evildoers wanted to impose on you to kill the fire of faith in your hearts. . . .

God is great; God is great; may the lowly be defeated. Victory is sweet with the help of God.

The coalition calls upon the Iraqi Government to designate military commanders to meet within 48 hours with their coalition counterparts at a place in the theater of operations to be specified to arrange for military aspects of the cease-fire.

Further, I have asked Secretary of State [James A. J. Baker] to request that the United Nations Security Council meet to formulate the necessary arrangement for this war to be ended.

Truce Depends on Iraq

This suspension of offensive combat operations is contingent upon Iraq's not firing upon any coalition forces and launching Scud missiles against any other country. If Iraq violates these terms, coalition forces will be free to resume military operations.

At every opportunity I have said to the people of Iraq that our quarrel was not with them but instead with their leadership and above all with Saddam Hussein. This remains the case. You, the people of Iraq, are not our enemy. We do not seek your destruction. We have treated your POWs with kindness.

Coalition forces fought this war only as a last resort and look forward to the day when Iraq is led by people prepared to live in peace with their neighbors.

Looking Beyond Victory

We must now begin to look beyond victory in war. We must meet the challenge of securing the peace. In the future, as before, we will consult with our coalition partners.

We've already done a good deal of thinking and planning for the post-war period, and Secretary Baker has already begun to consult with our coalition partners on the region's challenges. There can be and will be no solely American answer to all these challenges, but we can assist and support the countries of the region and be a catalyst for peace.

In this spirit Secretary Baker will go to the region next week to begin a new round of consultations. This war is now behind us. Ahead of us is the difficult task of securing a potentially historic peace. Tonight though, let us be proud of what we have accomplished. Let us give thanks to those who risked their lives. Let us never forget those who gave their lives.

May God bless our valiant military forces and their families and let us all remember them in our prayers.

Good night and may God bless the United States of America.

Here you see the power of primary documents once again. Accounts like these make history real in a way nothing else can. The selections make clear once more, however, that historians who view these records need to analyze them in depth. Many primary documents studied by scholars in American history are just as powerful, descriptive, interesting—and biased—as these. Careful study and the right questions help to separate fact from fiction.

Look at Hussein's and Bush's speeches again. Analyze the two sets using the critical questions of historical analysis listed below. Compare your responses with the suggested responses.

1. Who are the sources of the material?

2. Can the sources be verified? How?

3. Are the sources reliable?

4. What information is presented?

5. Can the information be verified?

6. What is the frame of reference for each?

7. What points of view are expressed?

8. Which parts of the account appear to be statements of fact?

9. Which parts appear to be statements of opinion?

10. What is the purpose of each account?

11. What appears to be the tone of each text?

You may have access to *Enduring Voices,* the document sets that accompany *The Enduring Vision,* or your professor may provide other primary documents. Your college library also has thousands of documents available. As interesting as these documents may be, remember that their deeper value lies in your ability to evaluate them as a historian. Your own frame of reference will play an important role in your analysis of historical data, and your awareness of how this framework affects your perception is crucial. From your own past experiences, you will bring valuable meaning to the material as you study. In addition, your history course will encourage you to *ask the questions* and search for meaning within the historical frame of reference. In so doing, you will join the authors and your instructor in the critical-thinking process.

SUGGESTED RESPONSES to Discussion 5

Application 5:

1. *Who are the sources of the material?* The *sources* of the material are Saddam Hussein, leader of Iraq, and George Bush, former president of the United States. The excerpts come from speeches given before the peoples of Iraq and the United States, respectively.

2. *Can the sources be verified? How?* The sources can be *verified* by checking public documents for the full accounts. The full text of Bush's speeches were recorded and documented in writing at the time they were given. Hussein's speeches were recorded and transcribed and translated as they were broadcast in Iraq.

3. *Are the sources reliable?* Both sources are considered *reliable* in the sense that they are authoritative figures assuming responsibility for the events that occurred.

4. *What information is presented?* Each account presents information concerning the causes and outcome of the war.

5. *Can the information be verified?* Even though the documents differ in perspective, we can verify the information that they present through other documents, such as records of troop placements and movements and independent observations of other witnesses.

6. *What is the frame of reference for each?* Hussein's *frame of reference* is that of a dictator of a militarily aggressive and powerful Muslim country in the Middle East. His religious orientation is obvious throughout the text of his speeches. Bush's frame of reference is that of a president of a militarily powerful country with ties to Christianity. He expresses his religious orientation as he ends each speech.

7. *What points of view are expressed?* Each set of speeches represent entirely opposite *points of view.* Hussein declares that Kuwait is an integral part of Iraq and that the taking of Kuwait is justified. His point of view is that Kuwait has been reunited with its mother country. He perceives the allies as aggressors who had no right to interfere with Iraq's "just" cause. In the second excerpt, Hussein defends the point of view that Iraq won the Gulf War.

President Bush expresses the point of view that allied intervention was necessary to return Kuwait to a state of independence from Iraq. He perceives Iraq as an aggressor who had no right to invade Kuwait, and he deplores the methods used by Hussein to take control of Kuwait. In the second excerpt, Bush expresses the point of view that the allies won the war.

8. *Which parts of the account appear to be statements of fact?* The statements of *fact* presented in each excerpt are those pertaining to the actual occupation of Kuwait, the destruction that occurred in Kuwait, the movements of troops, the U.N. resolutions, and the war's final outcome. Even though these statements are represented differently in each account, we could verify them by consulting other records and accounts.

9. *Which parts appear to be statements of opinion?* The statements of *opinion* are many. Hussein's references to Bush as an enemy of God and his statements concerning the "repugnant siege" that had "been led in evil and aggression by the machine and the criminal entity of America and its major allies. . . ." are example enough. Bush expresses an opinion when he refers to "Saddam Hussein's efforts to destroy completely Kuwait and its people." In his second speech, he says, "This is a victory for the United Nations, for all mankind, for the rule of law and for what is right." This is a statement of opinion, and certainly one with which Hussein would disagree.

10. *What is the purpose of each account?* The *purpose* of each speech is to persuade and inform. To an American point of view, Hussein's speeches appear to focus on persuasion, and Bush's speeches seem to have the purpose of informing. However, each in its own way is equally persuasive and informative. It is important that we see them in this way, for it is easy to let our own points of view interfere. Many of us might view Hussein's speeches as misinformation designed to mislead the Iraqi people. Remember, however, that the Iraqi people reading Bush's speeches might judge his words similarly. To think historically and critically, you must step outside your own frame of reference and point of view and try to analyze documents with as open a mind as possible.

11. *What appears to be the tone of each text?* The *tone* of the documents differs dramatically. Hussein's speeches are more aggressive and openly derogatory toward his enemies. His use of religious references to call his troops to arms, to enlist the support of the Iraqi people, and to defend his actions reveal how tone affects our perception of words. The tone of Bush's speeches is somewhat more subdued, and built on reason rather than emotion. Yet emotional appeal is not lacking. Bush also uses religious references that help to set the tone of his messages.

The differences in tone make it difficult to analyze the purpose in these examples. Because we are outside the Iraqi frame of reference, it is hard for us to understand Hussein's intent and message in the same way that the Iraqi people would.

DISCUSSION 6: Secondary Sources

Secondary sources differ from primary sources in that they are interpretations of events written by people who did not personally witness the events. Historians use secondary sources to find information about past events and to verify primary sources. Examples of secondary sources include history books, newspaper accounts, analytical interpretations by experts or scholars, and interpretations or summaries of historical information by history textbook authors. In this sense, *The Enduring Vision* is an example of a secondary source.

Because secondary documents are written by human beings, they pose the same problems as primary documents, and historians read them in much the same way. Remember, all writers are products of their times. Their interpretations "grow" from their own frames of reference and points of view and purposes. Historians must ask the same critical questions about validity, frame of reference, point of view, and purpose and tone to evaluate secondary sources as they do to weigh primary documents. By the same token, you must analyze the information presented in your history text by the standards used to evaluate all secondary historical sources.

Your history professor has chosen *The Enduring Vision* as a reliable source of information. He or she may ask you to conduct historical research to verify some accounts, and will supplement the text with lectures and class discussions. Your instructor may also provide additional information and alternate views, as well as offer his or her analysis about the text. All of these resources are valuable sources of historical information, and are well worth sharing with classmates and professors.

Suitability and Reliability

In judging the suitability and reliability of a secondary source, a historian asks whether the writer is an expert in a relevant field. Is the author an appropriate authority to provide an accurate account or interpretation? For example, the writings of a newspaper reporter who has attended only one White House press conference and who has no background in government studies will differ markedly from those of a reporter who has followed the political process through many administrations and who has an advanced degree in political science. The Gulf War writings of a prominent business leader will probably have a different emphasis from the record of a famous army general. Each author might offer something of value: the business leader, a perceptive analysis of the Gulf War's impact on the economy; the general, an account of military preparation and combat strategy for the war. A historian would consult one of these sources over the other, depending on the particular aspect of the war that is of interest. Assessing the suitability and reliability of secondary documents is a crucial part of critical analysis.

> **NOTE:**   Understandably, you may have difficulty determining the reliability and suitability of secondary sources at this stage. However, you *can* ask the historian's questions discussed on page 29 and use judgment in evaluating the documents. If you are working on a research project and are uncertain about the reliability and suitability of your sources, ask your professor for guidance.

Historians study secondary sources to search for threads of truth. They then summarize and interpret the information they find. Obviously, no scholar, no matter how industrious, could read all the primary and secondary sources covering all the important events in American history. Most historians thus specialize in one area of study in American history and rely on other specialists to provide scholarly interpretations and summaries that, once brought together, form a complete representation of United States history. Most American history textbooks have several authors, each of whom has researched his or her own area thoroughly.

Supporting Evidence

To analyze both secondary sources and primary documents, you need to evaluate the author's supporting evidence. In well-written material in which the author expresses a point of view, an opinion, or a conclusion, the writer offers supporting evidence for the statement. This evidence aims to help you to understand or to persuade you to accept the author's ideas. In most cases, supporting evidence combines these two intents. The critical reader analyzes the author's supporting evidence for purpose, reliability, and suitability. The critical reader also asks not only *what* the author has to say and what conclusions the author has reached, but also *how* the author uses evidence to back his or her statements. What information is offered in support of the author's conclusions? Is the evidence accurate? What appear to be assumptions, or suppositions, made by the author as he or she reached conclusions? What assumptions and inferences does the author expect the reader to make? (See Part III, Discussion 6, for more on inference and assumption.) Does the evidence directly relate to the issue at hand? Does the evidence lead the reader to the conclusions expressed by the author? What kind of supporting evidence is offered? What pieces of evidence may have been left out?

The critical reader asks questions about supporting evidence based on the kind of information presented. This is a fundamental skill that comes with practice and patience.

APPLICATION 6A: In Discussions 2 and 3, you worked with Mary Rowlandson's manuscript as a primary document written by an Indian captive during King Philip's War in New England in the late 1600s. For more background information concerning King Philip's War, turn to page 48 of this guide and read the textbook passage "Expansion and Native Americans" before you begin this exercise.

The following passage is an excerpt about King Philip's War from a secondary source, *The Invasion of America: Indian, Colonialism, and the Cant of Conquest.* The author is historian Francis Jennings. Read the passage and answer the questions that follow. Compare your answers with the suggested responses at the end of Discussion 6.

Excerpt 1:

The war then begun has been misnamed King Philip's War; it was, in fact, the Second Puritan Conquest. The standard way to characterize this famous event has been to call it a racial showdown. This, too, is wrong. Far from having any unity of contestants, this explosion resembled on a smaller scale and in a shorter span the Thirty Years' War in Europe. It became a congeries of conflicts of which the resistance led by Wampanoag sachem Philip was only one. Different Europeans pursued different interests and fought different conflicts, and so did different Indians. (p. 298)

Excerpt 2:

To say that the war was not one of racial survival or racial extermination is not to say that individual episodes of the conflict lacked the quality of total war. There was carnage and atrocity to surfeit, committed by both sides, but neither the English general populace (apart from its bellicose rulers) nor the Indians in general entered willingly upon the war. Showing no consciousness whatever that racial survival was at stake, militiamen of Massachusetts and Plymouth energetically dodged impressment. To create an adequate military force the authorities had to resort to employment of piratical mercenaries, threats of punishment, and promises of plunder.

On the Indian side the record is quite clear about the bulk of involvement; in spite of the standard rumoring of conspiracies (never supported by substantial evidence), the first mobilizations

and the first attacks were made by Puritans. (p. 299)

As in the case of the Rowlandson manuscript in Discussion 1, short excerpts such as these do not give a complete picture of the original document. There is not enough space here to do justice to Jennings's efforts to explain and support his interpretations. For further study, consult the pertinent passages from Jennings's book, which will give you the complete details of this scholarly account.

Because you do not have access to the full text, some of the questions below will be difficult to answer. If you feel that you do not have enough information to answer a question, note that as your response and go on to the other questions. Full explanations are provided in the suggested responses.

1. What is the source of the material?

2. Can the source be verified? How?

3. Is the source reliable?

4. What information is presented?

5. Can the information be verified?

6. What appears to be the author's frame of reference?

7. What points of view are expressed?

8. What conclusions does the author present?

9. How are these conclusions supported?

10. Which parts of the document appear to be statements of fact?

11. Which parts appear to be statements of opinion?

12. What is the purpose of the account?

13. What appears to be the tone in the account?

APPLICATION 6B: The excerpts below come from Jeffrey Record, *Hollow Victory: A Contrary View of the Gulf War* (Brassey's, 1993). Read the passages, asking yourself the questions for analysis of secondary sources. Look especially for fact and opinion, purpose and tone. Then compare your responses with the suggested responses.

Excerpt 1:

It is far from clear, however, whether the Bush administration would have been satisfied with a resolution of the Kuwait crisis short of war. A voluntary Iraqi withdrawal from Kuwait would have satisfied the major declared political objective of the U.S.-led coalition, though it would have left Iraqi military power intact and Saddam himself (presumably) still in control of Iraq's destiny. The White House clearly harbored intentions against Iraq—the dictator's removal and his country's disarmament—that not only exceeded any strict interpretation of the U.N. mandate, but also, given Saddam's seemingly mindless intransigence from

August 2, 1990, to January 16, 1991, could be accomplished only by war. This disparity between more limited formal objectives and ambitious, undeclared aims continues to hamper attempts at judging the war's ultimate success or failure. (p. 2)

Excerpt 2:

The abyss in military prowess separating the two sides makes it very difficult to draw meaningful lessons for the future. Was the Coalition really that good, or the Iraqi military so awful? What are the chances of ever again encountering so incompetent an opponent in the Third World? Was the war really a meaningful test of U.S. military effectiveness, given Iraqi weaknesses and stupidity, to say nothing of the unusually favorable political, operational, topographical, and climatological conditions both Desert Shield and Desert Storm enjoyed? Could a more worldly, intelligent, and enterprising Iraqi leadership have derailed Desert

Storm, or at least raised its cost in blood to politically unacceptable levels for the United States? Was it really a war, or little more than a live-fire exercise? Was it a harbinger of future U.S. military interventions, or a singular, aberrational event devoid of useful lessons for the future? And what lessons from the Gulf War are being drawn by other countries, especially other aspiring, regional hegemonies with ambitions at odds with U.S. security interests, including a now vengeful Saddam Hussein? What worked in the Persian Gulf that didn't in Korea and Indochina? What difference, for example, did the Cold War's demise make? (p. 7)

Excerpt 3:

The author believes that Saddam's survival and postwar behavior—and U.S. and allied inability to compel his compliance with the U.N. cease-fire's provisions or to remove the dictator altogether—must be counted as a

major American political defeat, given the enormity of the international diplomatic, political, and military effort marshaled against him during and after the Gulf War. (p. 8)

APPLICATION 6C: Read the excerpt below on "Operation Desert Storm" from *The Enduring Vision*. As you read, ask yourself the historian's questions listed in Application 6A. Compare your answers to the suggested responses.

Operation Desert Storm

On August 2, 1990, Iraq invaded its neighbor, the oil-rich sheikdom of Kuwait. with which it had a long-running dispute over the vast Rumaila oilfield. Iraq's dictator,

Saddam Hussein, had dismissed Kuwait's independent-nation status as a creation of Western imperialists and asserted Iraq's historic claims to the region.

Under Saddam, Iraq for years had threatened not only Israel but the Arab nations as well. The Iraqi military buildup, including both chemical- and nuclear-weapons programs, had worried many governments in the 1980s.

During the Iran-Iraq war that had raged from 1980 to 1988, however, the United States had tilted in Iraq's favor because Iran was rabidly anti-American. But Iranian hostility to the United States moderated after the death of Ayatollah Khomeini in 1989, so this incentive to placate Iraq was removed. When Iraq invaded Kuwait, Washington immediately denounced the act.

Avoiding the mistakes of Lyndon Johnson in the Vietnam era, Bush built a consensus for action against Iraq in the Congress, in the United Nations, and among the American people. He also articulated a clear military objective — Iraq's withdrawal from Kuwait — and deployed more than 40,000 troops in Saudi Arabia to achieve that goal. Secretary of Defense Dick Cheney, formerly a Wyoming congressman, played a key role in this effort.

A series of U.N. resolutions imposed economic sanctions against Iraq and insisted that Saddam withdraw from Kuwait by January 15, 1991. On January 12, after somber debate, the Senate and the House endorsed military action against Iraq. The vote was 52 to 47 in the Senate; 250 to 183 in the House. Most Democrats voted against war, favoring continued economic sanctions instead.

The war began on January 16 with a massive and sustained air assault. For nearly six weeks, U.S. B-52 and F-16 bombers, flying up to 3,000 sorties daily, pounded Iraqi troops in the field, Iraqi supply depots, and command and communications targets in Iraq's capital, Baghdad. The air forces of other nations participated as well.

Although Iraq offered little direct resistance to this air attack, Saddam ordered Soviet-made Scud missiles fired against Tel Aviv and other Israeli cities, as well as against the Saudi capital, Riyadh. These did little damage, but Americans watched transfixed as the Cable News Network carried live coverage of U.S. Patriot missiles streaking off to intercept incoming Scuds.

Indeed, for Americans viewing a carefully edited version of the war on TV, it often seemed a glorified video game. The reality of an estimated 100,000 Iraqi deaths, both military and civilian, hardly impinged on the national consciousness.

On February 23, after diversionary maneuvers to mislead Iraqi commanders, 200,000 U.S. troops under General H. Norman Schwarzkopf moved across the desert toward Kuwait. Although heavy rains turned the roadless sands to soup, the army ground on. Within three days Iraqi soldiers were in full flight or surrendering en masse. U.S. forces destroyed 3,700 Iraqi tanks while losing only three. One hundred hours after the ground war had begun, with Iraqi resistance crushed, President Bush declared a cease-fire. After U.S. forces liberated Kuwait City, members of Kuwait's ruling al-Sabah family gradually filtered back from Cairo and other safe havens where they had sat out the war. Total American casualties numbered 148 dead — including 35 killed inadvertently by U.S. firepower — and 467 wounded.

As the victory celebrations receded, the war's political aftermath came into focus. Kuwait expelled many thousands of Palestinian laborers for their support of Iraq, creating a major refugee problem. Within Iraq, amid widespread civilian hardship and malnutrition, Saddam still held power. His army brutally suppressed uprisings against his rule by Shiite Muslims in the south and a large Kurdish ethnic minority in the north. United Nations inspectors found convincing evidence of Iraq's advanced nuclear-weapons project, and the halting of this sinister undertaking was viewed with general relief. (pp. 1061–1062)

As you have seen in Part II, all historical data, both primary and secondary, must be analyzed thoroughly before historians use it and can be accepted only when compared with many other primary and secondary sources. Moreover, all authors write from within a particular frame of reference. Their writing will reflect their points of view. Their purpose will be indicated by tone. Their word choice will shape their presentation of fact and opinion. Their assumptions and inferences will affect their interpretations and their decisions to include or omit information. Critical readers keep these facts in mind as they question and analyze what they read.

SUGGESTED RESPONSE to Discussion 6

Application 6A:

1. *What is the source of the material?* The source of the material is a reputable historian. If the full text were available to you, you would find that the author provides a list of references, or a bibliography, to back up the information presented. Such a list contains both primary and secondary sources.

2. *Can the source be verified? How?* The sources can be verified through research of other primary and secondary documents.

3. *Is the source reliable?* The reliability of the sources could be researched to determine whether the source is an expert in this particular area of study.

4. *What information is presented?* The author presents information about the conflict known as King Philip's War. The author asserts that the war was really a series of separate conflicts and that the Puritans attacked first.

5. *Can the information be verified?* This information could be partially verified by other authorities in the field. However, much of the excerpted material shown in this sample represents *interpretation* and would be difficult to verify with complete certainty.

6. *What appears to be the author's frame of reference?* The author's frame of reference is historical and academic.

7. *What points of view are expressed?* The author's points of view are that the Puritans started the conflict and that the war was not fought for purposes of racial extinction.

8. *What conclusions does the author present?* The author's conclusions are as follows:

King Philip's War was misnamed because it really was not a war in the conventional sense of the word, but instead a series of separate conflicts taken together.

The characterization of the war as a fight for racial extinction or survival was determined later. Those who fought the war did not view the conflict this way.

Neither the Indians nor the English really desired an all-out war.

The Puritans attacked first, and the rumors concerning Indian conspiracies were false.

9. *How are these conclusions supported?* In the excerpts, you will find very little support for the author's conclusions. Actually, the remainder of the chapter from which they were taken offers supporting evidence for each of these conclusions. However, in the second excerpt, the author offers a statement about the hiring of mercenaries to support his conclusion that the colonists did not want to fight. The important thing to recognize is that the excerpts contain little or no evidence. Therefore, you would proceed with caution in accepting the author's conclusions at face value.

10. *Which parts of the document appear to be statements of fact?* Statements of fact by this author that could be verified by other sources include those concerning the hiring of mercenaries by the Puritans and the first attacks.

11. *Which parts appear to be statements of opinion?* The excerpts contain many statements of opinion. These range from the comments concerning the misnaming of the war, the reasons for the conflicts, and both sides' feelings about the fighting.

12. *What is the purpose of the account?* The author's purpose appears to be to inform and persuade.

13. *What appears to be the tone in the account?* The tone suggests that the author wants to disprove standard assumptions about a historical event.

Application 6B:

1. *What is the source of the material?* The author of these passages is Jeffrey Record, a U.S. Senate aide. He has served as legislative assistant to Senator Sam Nunn and has been a columnist for the *Baltimore Sun,* as well as a policy analyst at the Brookings Institution, the Institute for Foreign Policy Analysis, the Hudson Institute, and BDM International. He has written many articles commenting on political and defense matters.

2. *Can the source be verified? How?* Yes, because these excerpts were taken from the original publication of his book. However, the real question lies in determining whether the references that he uses can be verified. Record does identify other sources and has included a bibliography that could be checked.

3. *Is the source reliable?* Is Record an "expert" in the field? Because the author is a well-known journalist on matters of political and defense analyses, some would recognize his credentials as suitable for commentary on the Persian Gulf War. However, he is not a recognized historical scholar, so a historian might well question his analysis. Therefore, the suit-

ability of this source raises questions; historians would probably consider the book only when used in conjunction with other secondary documents offering interpretations of the Gulf War.

4. *What information is presented?* The author offers his analysis of the effectiveness of the Gulf War.

5. *Can the information be verified?* Yes, the analysis is presented in an original publication.

6. *What is the author's frame of reference?* The author's frame of reference is that of a contemporary political analyst, not a historical scholar.

7. *What point of view is expressed?* The author's point of view as shown in the excerpts above appears to be that there were more reasons for the war than U.S. officials overtly expressed and that the idea of victory at the end of the war is questionable.

8. *What conclusions does the author present?* The author presents a series of conclusions relating to his points of view that the U.S. government had a hidden agenda in declaring war on Iraq and that the U.S. declaration of victory at the end of the war is not accurate.

9. *How are these conclusions supported?* In the first two excerpts, the author presents no supporting evidence. Each statement is one of assumption and/or inference. In excerpt 3, the author supports his thesis that the United States did not achieve victory in the Gulf War. He does so by calling attention to the fact that Hussein still held power and after the war still ignored the United Nations' mandates. If we examine this evidence for suitability, we find that in order to accept it as proof of U.S. political defeat, we must also accept Record's other unsupported conclusions concerning the hidden agenda of the U.S. government. According to Record, the agenda stipulated the total defeat and removal of Hussein from power. If we do not accept this author's initial assumptions concerning U.S. motives for the war, we cannot accept his evidence concerning defeat at the end of the war.

10. *Which parts of the excerpts appear to be fact?* In excerpt 3, the idea that Saddam survived and retained power in Iraq is factual.

11. *Which parts appear to be opinion?* All of the material presented in these excerpts falls into the category of opinion. The author presents an interpretation of events and identifies them clearly as his own opinions by indicating that he is providing an analysis.

12. *What is the purpose of the account?* The author's purpose is to inform and persuade. He presents his opinions, interpretations, and conclusions. In the full text, Record supports these opinions with many kinds of evidence. The account provides excellent practice for anyone interested in analyzing suitability of evidence and the use of assumption to build hypotheses.

13. *What is the author's tone?* The tone is one of skepticism, of questioning the overtly stated causes and conclusions of the Gulf War. As Record questions, his tone indicates his intent to negate the war's causes and conclusions that the government would have us believe. Wording such as "harbored intentions against," "disparity between," "undeclared aims," and the author's use of questioning in the second excerpt reveal his tone.

Application 6C:

1. *What is the source of the material?* The source of this passage is an author of *The Enduring Vision,* 3rd ed.

2. *Can the source be verified? How?* The source can be verified as original material in an accepted history text. Because the text lists multiple authors but does not designate which author wrote which section of the text, we could contact the publisher with further inquiries about the author of this particular passage. Also, given that the text is a secondary source, we would consult the bibliography at the end of the chapter to determine the validity of the author's sources.

3. *Is the source reliable?* The source can be considered reliable as a well-known historian in his or her field of study. We would also need to consider the reliability of the author's sources as listed in the bibliography.

4. *What information is presented?* This passage presents information and analyses of events pertaining to the 1991 Persian Gulf War.

5. *Can the information be verified?* We can verify information concerning Operation Desert Storm by consulting primary documents such as government and military records and eyewitness accounts. Secondary sources such as news accounts and editorial commentaries can be analyzed for supporting evidence for the primary documentation.

6. *What appears to be the author's frame of reference?* The author's frame of reference is that of a historical scholar. The manner in which the material is presented also indicates a generally pro-Western frame of reference.

7. *What points of view are expressed?* Within the pro-Western frame of reference, the author expresses points of view concerning reasons for the changing U.S. attitude toward Iraq and Iran before the war, Bush's support from Congress and the American public before and during the war, the American public's reaction to news coverage of the war, and the successful conclusion to the military actions of the United States.

8. *What conclusions does the author present?* The author appears to conclude that Bush had congressional and public support for his military response to the Iraqi seizure of Kuwait. (We infer this point from the contrast made to Johnson's mistakes in the Vietnam era.) The author also seems to conclude that the U.S. military accomplished an overwhelming victory and "crushed" Iraqi resistance in a very short time, that the American public was generally unconcerned with the death and destruction imposed on the enemy, that the news coverage was controlled by the U.S. government, and that the United States was successful in halting the Iraqis' advanced nuclear-weapons project.

9. *How are these conclusions supported?* The author supports conclusions of congressional and public support for military action by describing Bush's and Cheney's successful efforts to gain U.N. sanctions and a congressional vote to proceed with military intervention. We might question this author's supporting evidence concerning public support because, given constraints of length, limited information is provided about the ambiguous

response from Congress and the American public. The author on the other hand supports conclusions of U.S. victory with detailed information and statistics concerning the military confrontation and the withdrawal of the Iraqi army. The author's statement that Iraqi resistance was "crushed" is not explicitly supported by the evidence given and might be questioned. The author also offers no direct support for the conclusion that the Iraqi nuclear-weapons capability was halted, although we can infer that the nuclear effort was checked as a result of the war's devastation.

10. *Which parts of the document appear to be statements of fact?* Factual information includes dates and statistics. These can be verified by consulting other sources.

11. *Which parts appear to be statements of opinion?* This author expresses opinion throughout the passage in sections containing interpretations and conclusions. A paragraph from p. 1061 demonstrates this author's statements of opinion: "Indeed, for Americans viewing a carefully edited version of the war on TV, it often seemed a glorified video game. The reality of an estimated 100,000 Iraqi deaths, both military and civilian, hardly impinged on the national consciousness."

12. *What is the purpose of the account?* The author's purpose appears to be to inform and to describe. However, an element of persuasion can be inferred from the author's tone.

13. *What appears to be the tone of the author?* The author's tone is indicated in the manner in which information and descriptions are worded. The author states that Iran was "rabidly" anti-American in order to explain why the United States supported Iraq in its war with Iran and that this was "an incentive to placate Iraq." The paragraph shown in response 11 above contains several phrases that signal tone, such as "seemed a glorified video game," and "hardly impinged on the national consciousness." The author refers to "brilliant maneuvers to mislead Iraqi commanders" and "Iraqi resistance crushed." Saddam's army "brutally suppressed uprisings" in Iraq. The author uses the word *sinister* to describe Iraq's weapons program.

The author of this passage concludes with the statement, "Nevertheless, by early 1992, the Gulf War seemed more distant, and feelings about it more mixed, than anyone could have predicted a year before." This sentence appears to refer to the fiery debate still going on in the United States about Hussein's retention of power, his refusal to submit to U.N. inspections of military sites, and his continuing military threat to the Middle East.

PART III

Critical Reading: The Reading Process

Part III gives you some handy tools, such as previewing your text, identifying a passage's central theme, and concept mapping, that will help you to read and understand *The Enduring Vision*. In fact, these tools are so versatile that you can use them to read any written material for meaning, not just a history text. As you master these skills, you'll find yourself dissecting complicated textbook passages with ease, remembering the key ideas, and building the foundation of information that you'll use again and again in school and life.

Understanding the Reading Process

The basic purpose of reading well is so simple that we might easily forget or ignore it. Writers write in order to share a message with their readers; readers read to understand the writer's message. For this communication process to succeed, writers and readers rely on certain essentials, commonly called conventions, of writing. Together, these conventions provide the base on which all written material is built. Your success as a reader depends on your ability to use this base to your advantage when you read and study any written communication. Textbooks, journal and newspaper articles, literature, business communications, manuals, and many other forms of written material are constructed using guidelines that help you to follow the author's thoughts.

Understanding Writing Conventions as Reading Tools

Writers construct sets of paragraphs, called passages, to convey their ideas to you, the reader. Each passage contains a central theme, the primary message that the author wants you to understand. Each paragraph within a passage contains one main idea that relates to and helps explain the central theme. Each paragraph also has several sentences that relate to and explain the paragraph's main idea.

By understanding the guidelines behind the construction of written material, you can take apart passages and paragraphs to read for meaning. You will understand the author's central theme and main ideas and be able to judge the relative importance of details and critically evaluate the passage. You will also be able to summarize and paraphrase important ideas and see the connections between these ideas and the author's overall message. All of these skills are basic to gaining the knowledge you need to be a successful student. You not only will understand what you read, but also be better able to remember and apply your knowledge to new challenges.

The process is surprisingly simple and is built on a system of questioning while reading. The experienced reader knows which questions to ask and when to ask them.

> **NOTE:**   The first two sets of exercises in this section ask you to survey your textbook and preview an individual chapter. Have your textbook handy in order to get the most out of these exercises. References are intended for the complete textbook, *The Enduring Vision*, 3rd ed., (Boyer et al.). If you have a shorter version of the textbook in paperback form, the exercises are still appropriate but may need to be adjusted for small differences in format.

DISCUSSION 1: Surveying Your Textbook

In order to read for meaning, you should first get a broad overview of the book. A general survey, or preview, of your textbook will give you "the big picture" of the organizational patterns the authors use, the range of information they cover, and the aids to understanding they provide. You will find that *The Enduring Vision* uses a unique "building-block" narrative format that is both interesting and informative. The authors apply the conventions of writing to tell a vivid, thought-provoking story that will engage and surprise you. The many maps and illustrations, and the features such as "A Place in Time," will help you not only to understand but also to enjoy reading about the United States' past.

> **NOTE:**   In surveying assigned textbook material before you begin reading, resist the temptation to skip this stage to save time; with practice, previewing the material becomes more automatic and less time consuming. By spending a few minutes preparing to read, you will save time and energy later.

APPLICATION 1:   To survey your text, follow the steps below.

1. Look at *The Enduring Vision*'s title page and list of authors. Read the material at the beginning of the book that gives information about the authors and their credentials. Skim the Preface. The Preface contains notes to the instructor, mentions materials designed to supplement the text, and gives credit to the scholars who have reviewed and edited the information in the text. This section gives you a sense of the text's credibility.

2. On the back of the title page, find the copyright date of your textbook. Always check the copyright date of any material you read. To evaluate the contents of a textbook, it is important to know whether the information is current. Because *The Enduring Vision* has a recent copyright date, you may reasonably assume that the contents are up-to-date.

3. Look at the maps on the inside front and back covers of your text. Note the information they present. You will refer to these often as you read.

4. Look at the Table of Contents. Skim the chapter and section headings to see how material is organized. Remember that your purpose here is to get an overview of the text's organizational pattern. Don't get overwhelmed or bogged down at this point. You won't be expected to read the entire textbook overnight! At the end of the Table of Contents, note the material listed under the Epilogue and Appendix sections. Following the Table of Contents, notice that a list of the textbook's maps appears. There are also pages that list charts, graphs, and tables. You will refer to these lists later during your reading.

5. Turn to the Appendix section at the end of the book. Notice what is presented here. Historical documents are provided for your reference. You will read these in depth as you reach sections in the textbook that discuss each document. Look through the remainder of the Appendix section to see what information is given in the charts. Knowing where these are in the textbook and using them as you need them will save you time and trouble.

6. Find the Index at the back of the book. This is the text's most valuable reference tool. As you read the chapters, you will often come across information that depends on knowledge of people and events mentioned in other sections of the textbook. If you are having trouble comprehending material, use the Index to look up explanatory information provided elsewhere in the textbook.

7. Turn to the Prologue, beginning on page xxxii. The Prologue provides a starting point for studying American history by giving a descriptive overview of the history of the land itself. Note the maps and illustrations. Skim this section, noting the section headings and the chronology at the end. You will return to the Prologue later and read it thoroughly.

Now ask yourself these questions:

1. What period or periods of history will I be studying?

2. How do the authors organize chapters and learning aids to help me gain a complete picture of these historical periods and the relationship of one period to another?

3. How might I best use the illustrations and format of the text to understand and remember what I read?

4. What use can I make of the Appendix and Index sections of this text while I am reading and reviewing?

As you answer these questions (and others that you may pose for yourself), you probably will realize what a valuable tool the survey method can be. Everyone has experienced that feeling of dread that sometimes comes when we brace ourselves to live day and night with a college textbook for a semester. After surveying the text, you might actually look forward to discovering what the book and your course have to offer.

DISCUSSION 2: Previewing a Chapter

Just as surveying a textbook can "jump-start" your reading, previewing a chapter gives you a sense for how the author intends to communicate broad ideas. A chapter preview works somewhat like a movie preview. As you skim through the various elements that make up the chapter, you get an overview of the whole picture. Previewing prepares you to read with understanding.

Practice previewing by following the procedures below. As you take these steps, remember that the goal is to gain an overview, to acquire a broad picture of the main issues, to see how the chapter is organized, and to preview the aids to understanding included in the chapter.

APPLICATION 2: Choose any chapter in *The Enduring Vision* and follow the steps below.

1. Look at the chapter title and reflect on its meaning. What can you expect to read about in this chapter?

2. Each chapter contains sections that focus on central topics. Read the section and sub-section titles to introduce yourself to the ideas that the author expects to cover. As you read these, ask yourself how these ideas relate to one another and to the chapter as a whole.

3. *The Enduring Vision* is filled with interesting and helpful illustrations such as pictures, charts, and maps. If you skipped over these while reading the section titles, look at them now. The illustrations have captions beside or beneath them. Skim the captions to see what the illustrations show, and ask yourself how they fit in with the section titles and subtitles.

   NOTE: Always include illustrations in your previewing, reading, and reviewing. Not only do they clarify the written material, they also provide additional information not covered in the narrative text.

4. At the beginning of each chapter, the authors provide a short introduction that focuses on one element of the chapter material to capture your interest and to provide background knowledge. Skim this section during the preview. Ask yourself how the material in the introduction relates to the chapter title and sections you have previewed.

5. Each chapter of *The Enduring Vision* also has a special two-page essay called, "A Place in Time." These essays provide an in-depth description of a particular community or society viewed during the time period discussed in the chapter. Like the introduction, the "Place in Time" essays aim to spark your interest and build your background knowledge; they also seek to deepen your understanding of relationships between people and events and bring the past alive. Skim the "Place in Time" feature in your chapter and be aware of its placement. As you read the chapter later, you will want to examine "A Place in Time" thoroughly. If you are not aware of the intended use of this section, its placement in the text may seem unusual. Don't be discouraged by this. The logical time to read this section will become apparent later when you read the chapter. As you look through "A Place in Time," ask what points the essay appears to cover and how it connects with the sections you have previewed.

6. At the end of the chapter, the authors offer a section called "Conclusion." In some chapters, the conclusion summarizes the main ideas covered in the chapter, but this is not always the case. Some conclusions recap the cultural problems of the chapter's

time period and provide the authors' interpretations. Based on your preview to this point, determine which of the above-mentioned functions the conclusion of your preview chapter appears to fulfill.

Read the chapter conclusion thoroughly to orient your thinking and to focus on the chapter's main concepts. Don't worry; your textbook is not intended to be read as a mystery novel. It's okay to read the end first. It's always helpful to know where you're headed before you start out.

7. Following the chapter conclusion is a chronology, a list of dates paired with various events and developments. Read the chronology to get an idea of the chapter's time frame and to gain exposure to important information. Don't worry about learning the dates now; they will make more sense after you read the chapter. Don't hesitate to turn to this list at any point in your reading if you need help keeping track of events. The list will also serve as a helpful review tool later.

8. Look at the sections at the end of the chapter titled "For Further Reading" and "Additional Bibliography." Your authors have listed other material to help you to research a topic. You may want to use these references to acquire background information or to read more about a topic that strikes you as particularly interesting. If your professor assigns a research project, these references provide a convenient starting point.

Managing Your Reading Time

After previewing your chapter, take a few minutes to plan the best way to read the chapter thoroughly. What are the logical divisions within the chapter? How many sections in each division can you read with interest and total attention at one sitting? How much reading time does your schedule allow, and how can you best ration that time? Look at your course syllabus. How has your instructor organized course lectures and reading assignments? How much of each chapter do you need to read in order to be prepared for each class?

The answers to these questions will differ for each individual. Be realistic, and plan your slots of uninterrupted reading time. By previewing the chapter and knowing what you need to cover, you will avoid last-minute surprises and frantic, late-night reading marathons.

Previewing the text creates a framework for comprehending what you read as you read it. Even though it takes a little time, it will save you much more time and effort in the long run. Previewing helps to keep you from having to read a chapter over and over. Try it. Practice it. It works!

DISCUSSION 3: Reading Textbook Passages

After surveying your textbook and previewing a chapter, you should have an idea of how the authors have organized the reading material. Now you are ready to begin seriously reading and analyzing chapter passages, or sections.

The best way to begin is to break the chapter and its sections down into smaller sections. *The Enduring Vision* authors have done this for you by providing subsections. Each subsection treats a central idea in depth, and your goal is to uncover that central theme.

Reading for the Central Theme

Discerning the central theme is the most essential element of reading for understanding. However, it can be the most difficult task to accomplish, for you will need to read an entire passage *without stopping, without marking the text,* and *without taking notes.* If you have learned in the past to underline or highlight as you read, you might find this step quite challenging.

In college reading, marking the text during the first reading of a passage can interfere with your comprehension. The temptation to mark details often causes a reader to lose sight of the central theme and main ideas. It is the central theme and main ideas that provide a coherent message. Once you understand the passage's overall message, the details will make more sense and fall into logical order. Experienced readers use the relationships among central theme, main ideas, and details as a foundation for taking notes and studying the material *after* their first reading.

APPLICATION 3:   This exercise shows you how to read a passage first for overall meaning. The questions will help you to focus on the passage's central theme or message.

Read the following passage, "Expansion and Native Americans," all the way through without stopping. To detect the passage's central theme, ask yourself:

1. What is the passage about? Answer this question in two or three words or a short phrase. (This is the TOPIC of the passage.)

2. What does the author intend for me to understand? What is the writer's message to me about the topic? Answer this question with a complete sentence. (This is the CENTRAL THEME of the passage.)

3. How does the author use historical data to explain his or her message? What general kind of supporting information does the author use to help me to understand the central theme? (These queries point to the DEVELOPMENT OF THE CENTRAL THEME.) Answer the questions with a few phrases. At this point, don't concern yourself with specific details.

After reading the passage and answering these questions, compare your responses with the suggested responses at the end of Discussion 3.

Expansion and Native Americans

As the settlers grew and prospered, the Native Americans declined. Although Indians began to recover from the initial epidemics by midcentury, the settlers brought new diseases such as diphtheria, measles, and tuberculosis, as well as new outbreaks of smallpox, that took heavy tolls. New England's Indian population had been reduced from 125,000 in 1600 to 10,000 in 1675.

Native Americans felt the English presence in other ways. The fur trade, which initially benefitted interior natives, became a burden after midcentury. Once Indians began hunting for trade instead of just for their own subsistence needs, they quickly depleted the beavers and other fur-bearing animals of the region. And because English traders customarily advanced trade goods on credit to Indian hunters before the hunting season, the lack of pelts pushed many natives into debt. In this situation traders such as John Pynchon of Springfield, Massachusetts, began taking Indian land as collateral and selling it to settlers.

Elsewhere, English townsmen, eager to expand their agricultural output and provide land for their sons, voted themselves much larger amounts of land after 1660 and insisted that their scattered parcels be consolidated. For example, Dedham, Massachusetts, which distributed only three thousand acres from 1636 to 1656, allocated five times as much in the next dozen years. Rather than continue living closely together, many farmers built homes on their outlying tracts, thereby coming into closer proximity to native settlements and the Indians' hunting, gathering, and fishing areas.

As the settlements expanded, they put new pressures on the natives and the land alike. As early as 1642, Miantonomi, a Narragansett sachem (chief), warned other New England Indians:

"These English having gotten our land, they with scythes cut down the grass, and with axes fell the trees; their cows and horses eat the grass, and their hogs spoil our clam banks, and we shall all be starved."

Within a generation, Miantonomi's fears were being borne out. By clearing away extensive stands of trees for fields and for use as fuel and building material, colonial farmers inadvertently altered an entire ecosystem. Deer were no longer attracted, and the wild plants upon which the Indians depended for food and medicine could not grow. The soil became drier

and flooding more frequent in the face of this deforestation. The settlers also introduced domestic livestock, which, according to English custom, ran wild. Pigs damaged Indian cornfields (until the natives adopted the alien practice of fencing their land) and shellfish gathering sites. English cattle and horses quickly devoured native grasses, which the settlers then replaced with English varieties.

With the native religious leaders, and their practices, powerless to halt the alarming decline of Indian population, land, and food sources, many Indians became demoralized. In their despair some turned to alcohol, increasingly available during the 1660s despite colonial efforts to suppress its sale to Native Americans. Interpreting the crisis as one of belief, others joined those Indians who had already converted to Christianity. By 1675 Puritan missionaries had established about thirty praying towns in eastern Massachusetts and Plymouth and on the islands of Martha's Vineyard and Nantucket. Supervised by missionaries, each praying town nevertheless had its own Native American magistrate, usually a sachem, and many praying congregations had Indian preachers. Although the missionaries struggled to convert the Indians to "civilization," by which they meant English culture and life-styles as well as to Christianity, most praying Indians integrated the new faith with their native cultural identities. This practice reinforced the hostility of most settlers, who believed that all Indians were irrevocably "savage" and heathen.

Anglo-Indian conflict became acute during the 1670s because of the pressure imposed on unwilling Indians to sell their land and to accept missionaries and the legal authority of colonial courts. Tension ran especially high in the Plymouth colony, where the English had engulfed the Wampanoags and forced a number of humiliating concessions on their leader, Metacom, or "King Philip," the son of Massasoit, the Pilgrims' onetime ally.

In 1675 Plymouth hanged three Wampanoags for killing a Christian Indian and threatened to arrest Metacom. A minor incident in which several Wampanoags were shot while burglarizing a farmhouse led to a steady escalation of violence; and Metacom soon organized about two-thirds of the Native Americans, including perhaps a third of all Christian Indians, into a military alliance. "But little remains of my ancestor's domain, I am resolved not to see the day when I have no country," Metacom declared as he and his followers ignited the conflict known as King Philip's War.

Metacom's forces—unlike the Indian combatants in the Pequot War, few of whom had fought with guns— were as well armed as the whites. The Indians attacked 52 of New England's 90 towns (of which 12 were entirely destroyed), burned 1,200 houses, slaughtered 8,000 head of cattle, and killed 600 colonists.

The tide turned against Metacom in 1676 after the Mohawk Indians of New York and many Christian Indians joined the English against him. English militiamen destroyed their enemies'

food supplies and sold hundreds of captives into slavery, including Metacom's wife and child. "It must have been as bitter as death to him," wrote Puritan clergyman Cotton Mather, "to lose his wife and only son, for the Indians are marvelously fond and affectionate toward their children." Perhaps three thousand Indians starved or fell in battle, including Metacom himself, and many more fled to New York and Canada.

King Philip's War reduced southern New England's Indian population by almost 40 percent and eliminated overt resistance to white expansion. It also deepened English hostility toward Native Americans, even the Christian Indians who fought Philip. In Massachusetts ten praying towns were disbanded and all Indians restricted to the remaining four; all Indian courts were dismantled; and "guardians" were appointed to supervise the reservations. "There is a cloud, a dark cloud upon the work of the Gospel among the poor Indians," mourned John Eliot. In the face of poverty and discrimination, remaining Indians managed to maintain their communities and cultural identities. To make up for the loss of traditional sources of sustenance, many worked as seamen or indentured servants, served in England's wars against the French in Canada, or made and sold baskets and other wares. (pp. 63–65)

SUGGESTED RESPONSES to Discussion 3:

Application 3:

1. TOPIC: The decline of American Indian population and culture.

2. CENTRAL THEME: The decline of American Indian population and culture stemmed from circumstances directly related to the expansion of European settlement as the number of Indians dwindled and their means for independent survival changed.

3. DEVELOPMENT OF CENTRAL THEME: The author develops the central theme by analyzing causes and effects. Specifically, expanded Anglo-European settlement caused the decline of American Indian culture. The author describes the effects of the expansion of white settlement on Indian life in detail. These effects range from loss of population due to disease and reduced hunting territory, to King Philip's War, which decimated the New England Indian tribes.

DISCUSSION 4: Reading Paragraphs

As we saw in Discussion 3, textbook authors use passages to develop a central theme. These long passages are made up of paragraphs, each of which develops a *main idea* that supports or explains the passage's central theme. To understand how writers group paragraphs to form messages about the passage's central theme, you need to dissect paragraphs to find their meaning.

Some paragraphs are easy to read. The main idea and supporting details seem to leap off the page at you. In these cases, there is no need to dissect each paragraph. You may have grown accustomed to reading material that lends itself to this somewhat automatic analysis. The challenge will be to learn to take apart more complex paragraphs.

College textbooks usually contain long, well-developed passages presenting complex concepts. The author explains these ideas within paragraphs full of supporting information. Not surprisingly, sorting through these complex, information-loaded materials can be a daunting task. Yet taking paragraphs apart (paragraph deconstruction) is *the most useful technique* for all reading, note taking, and studying. Indeed, dissecting paragraphs for meaning is the foundation of all reading comprehension and provides the essential tool for taking notes on textbook material.

Dissecting Paragraphs for Meaning

A paragraph is a series of sentences that work together to present or explain one idea about a single topic. To understand a paragraph, ask yourself:

1. What subject (topic) is the paragraph about?

2. What main idea does the author want me to understand about the topic?

3. How does the author support or explain that idea? What information does the author provide to help me to understand the idea?

APPLICATION 4A: Read the following paragraph with the above questions in mind, then compare your responses with the suggested responses at the end of Discussion 4.

West African societies changed with the coming of Portuguese slavers. In Guinea and Senegambia, which supplied the bulk of sixteenth-century slaves, small kingdoms expanded to "service" the trade. Some of their rulers became comparatively rich. Farther south, in present-day Angola, the kings of Kongo used the slave trade to consolidate their power and voluntarily adopted Christianity. Kongo flourished until the late sixteenth century, when attackers from the interior destroyed it. (p. 34).

Finding the Paragraph Topic

The first question that we discussed in the previous section asks about the paragraph subject or TOPIC. A well-written paragraph has only *one* topic, and every sentence in the paragraph relates to it.

APPLICATION 4B: In a paragraph, a topic "glues" all the sentences together. Read the paragraph below and determine the topic. To name the topic, use only two or three words or a short phrase. Compare your answer with the suggested response at the end of Discussion 4.

The Americas supplied seemingly limitless wealth for Spain. Not only did some Spaniards grow rich from West Indian sugar plantations and Mexican sheep and cattle ranches, but immense quantities of silver crossed the Atlantic after rich mines in Mexico and Peru began producing in the 1540s. A robust trade between America and Spain grew up, which Castilian officials tried to regulate. Spain took in far more American silver than its economy could absorb, setting off inflation that eventually engulfed all Europe. Bent on dominating Europe, the Spanish kings needed ever more American silver to pay their armies. Several times they went bankrupt, and their efforts to squeeze more taxes from their subjects provoked in the 1560s the revolt of Spain's rich Netherlands provinces—modern Belgium, Holland, and Luxemburg. In the end, gaining access to American wealth cost Spain dearly. (p. 39).

What is the paragraph TOPIC?

Finding the Paragraph's Main Idea

Authors write paragraphs to send a message to their readers about the paragraph topic. This message is called the paragraph's MAIN IDEA. A well-written paragraph contains only one main idea, and all the sentences in the paragraph relate to that idea. To find the main idea, ask what the author is trying to tell you about the paragraph topic.

APPLICATION 4C: Look again at the paragraph in Application 4B to see how this works. Reread the paragraph to determine the main idea. Remember that the paragraph TOPIC is *the effect of the Americas' wealth on Spain*. What is the author's MAIN IDEA about that topic? Write your answer in a complete sentence. Compare it with the suggested response at the end of Discussion 4.

Distinguishing Stated and Unstated Main Ideas

The main idea of a paragraph may be *stated* or *unstated*. In other words, the paragraph *may or may not* contain a sentence expressing the main idea. If the paragraph does contain such a sentence, we say that it has a *Topic Sentence* or a *Stated Main Idea*. This is true of the paragraph above. The last sentence of the paragraph states the main idea.

Sometimes the main idea is not presented in just one sentence in the paragraph. A combination of sentences may form the main idea, or you may have to *infer* the main idea from the paragraph's major details. In such cases, the main idea is *unstated*. You will need to grasp the writer's message by figuring out the idea common to all the sentences in the paragraph. Compare the following examples of stated and unstated main ideas.

Paragraph 1:

Tiny though they were, the Dutch and Swedish colonies were historically significant. New Netherland had attained a population of 9,000 and featured a wealthy, thriving port city by the time it came under English rule in 1664. Even short-lived New Sweden left a mark—the log cabin, that durable symbol of the American frontier, which Finnish settlers in the Swedish colony first introduced to the continent. Above all, the two colonies bequeathed an environment characterized by ethnic and religious diversity that would continue in England's "middle colonies." (p. 83).

TOPIC: The importance of the Dutch and Swedish colonies

***STATED* MAIN IDEA:**   The small Dutch and Swedish colonies were historically significant.

Paragraph 2:

The year 1864 proved crucial for the North. While Grant occupied Lee in the East, a Union army under William T. Sherman attacked from Tennessee into northwestern Georgia and took Atlanta in early September. The fall of Atlanta not only boosted northern morale but contributed to Lincoln's reelection. Now the curtain rose on the last act of the war. After taking Atlanta, Sherman marched across Georgia to Savannah, devastated the state's resources, and cracked its morale. Pivoting north from Savannah, Sherman then moved into South Carolina. Meanwhile, having backed Lee into trenches around Petersburg and Richmond, Grant forced the evacuation of both cities and brought on the Confederacy's collapse. (p. 491)

TOPIC: The collapse of the Confederacy

***UNSTATED* MAIN IDEA:**   In 1864 victories by the Union armies under Sherman and Grant brought about the final collapse of the Confederacy.

Paragraphs with topic sentences are relatively easy to understand—you need only recognize the main idea as presented in the author's words. If the main idea is unstated, however, you must express it in your own words. Even though this approach is more difficult, it is vital to learn not to depend on topic sentences. Instead, read through a paragraph and ask yourself the basic questions about topic and main idea: What subject is the paragraph about? What is the author trying to tell me about that subject? You can then check whether the paragraph has a sentence that states the main idea.

Readers who can express main ideas in their own words are better able to understand and remember what they read because they are reading for *ideas* rather than memorizing someone else's words.

APPLICATION 4D: Read each of the following paragraphs to identify the topic and main idea. Determine whether the main idea is stated or unstated. Compare your answers with our suggested responses at the end of Discussion 4.

Paragraph 1:

The War of 1812 had three major political consequences. First, it eliminated the Federalists as a national political force. Second, it went a long way toward convincing the Republicans that the nation was strong and resilient, capable of fighting a war while maintaining the liberty of its people. The third consequence was an outgrowth of the first two. With the Federalists tainted by disloyalty and with fears about the fragility of republics fading, Republicans increasingly embraced some doctrines long associated with the Federalists. In a message to Congress in December 1815, Madison called for federal support for internal improvements, tariff protection for the new industries that had sprung up during the embargo, and the creation of a new national bank. (The charter of the first Bank of the United States had expired in 1811.) In Congress another Republican, Henry Clay of Kentucky, proposed similar measures, which he called the American System, with the aim of making the nation economically self-sufficient and free from dependency on Europe. In 1816 Congress chartered the Second Bank of the United States and enacted a moderate tariff. Federal support for internal improvements proved to be a thornier problem. Madison favored federal aid in principle but believed that a constitutional amendment was necessary to authorize it. Accordingly, he vetoed an internal-improvements bill passed in 1817. (pp. 258–259)

What is the paragraph's TOPIC and MAIN IDEA? Is the main idea stated or unstated?

Paragraph 2:

New Englanders were not so fortunate. A short growing season and poor soil kept yields so low, even in the best of times, that farmers barely produced enough grain for local consumption. New Englanders also faced both high taxes to repay the money borrowed to finance the Revolution and a tightening of credit that spawned countless lawsuits against debtors. These problems had sparked Shays's Rebellion in 1786 and still defied solution. Whereas most southern states had largely eliminated their war debts and the Middle Atlantic states had made great progress in managing theirs, New England taxpayers remained under a crushing obligation. Economic depression only aggravated the region's chronic overpopulation. Young New England men continued migrating to the frontier or to the cities, and their discontent and restless mobility loosened the bonds of parental authority and left many women without marriage prospects. (p. 204)

What is the TOPIC and MAIN IDEA? Is the main idea stated or unstated?

Paragraph 3:

Within western families, there was usually a clear division of labor between men and women. Men performed most of the heaviest labor such as cutting down trees and plowing fields, but women had many chores. Women usually rose first in the morning, because their work included milking the cows as well as preparing breakfast. Women also fashioned the coverlets that warmed beds in unheated rooms, and prior to the spread of factory-made clothing in the 1830s, they made shirts, coats, pants, and dresses on home spinning wheels for family use. They often helped butcher hogs. They knew that the best way to bleed a hog was to slit its throat while it was still alive, and after the bleeding, they were adept at scooping out the innards, washing the heart and liver, and hanging them to dry. There was nothing dainty about the work of pioneer women. (p. 270)

What is the TOPIC and MAIN IDEA? Is the main idea stated or unstated?

SUGGESTED RESPONSES to Discussion 4:

Application 4A:

1. What is the paragraph about?

   West African slave trade.

2. What does the author want me to understand about the subject?

   West African societies changed and flourished from doing business with the Portuguese slave traders.

3. How does the author support or explain that idea?

   Guinea and Senegambia—small kingdoms expanded, rulers became richer because they helped Portuguese slavers.

   Angola—Kongo kings consolidated power because of slave trade and adopted Christianity.

Application 4B

TOPIC: The effect of the Americas' wealth on Spain

EXPLANATION: Every sentence in this paragraph relates in some way to the wealth that Spain took from America and the effects of that wealth on Spain. When a paragraph shows a clear pattern of development, like the cause/effect pattern of the above example, the topic often hints at the pattern. (For more on paragraph patterns, see Part III, Discussion 7.) Notice that the phrase expressing the topic is fairly specific. If we were to say only "wealth" or "Spain," the answer would be too general to be of any use. We need to name the topic with enough detail to capture the paragraph's focus.

Application 4C:

MAIN IDEA: Spain paid a high price to gain access to American wealth.

EXPLANATION: The last sentence of this paragraph is a topic sentence that states the main idea. The author's message to the reader is that Spanish access to riches from the Americas caused Spain many problems. Every sentence in the paragraph supports this idea.

Application 4D:

Paragraph 1:

TOPIC: Political consequences of the War of 1812.

MAIN IDEA: The War of 1812 had three major political consequences. (The first sentence of the paragraph is a *topic sentence* that *states* the main idea. The remainder of the paragraph's sentences support and explain this idea.)

Paragraph 2:

TOPIC: New England economy after the Revolution.

MAIN IDEA: New England's economy after the Revolution was depressed and had trouble regaining strength. (The main idea of paragraph 2 is *unstated*. We defined the main idea based on the sentences in the paragraph that give us reasons, causes, and consequences relating to New England's economic problems following the war.)

Paragraph 3:

TOPIC: The work of the pioneer women.

MAIN IDEA: In pioneer families, there was usually a clear division of labor between men and women; while men performed the heaviest labor, the women's work was difficult and demanding. (Normally, we could consider the first sentence of paragraph 3 to be a topic sentence. However, the author's emphasis on the kind of work performed by pioneer women leads us to conclude that the main message has more to do with the demanding work of pioneer women than a straightforward analysis of the division of labor in western families. This paragraph exemplifies the need to bring together all the information in a paragraph in order to determine the author's main idea.)

DISCUSSION 5: Identifying Major Details

A well-written paragraph contains a topic, a main idea about that topic, and several sentences that support or explain the main idea. Any information in a paragraph that *directly* supports or explains the main idea is called a MAJOR DETAIL. Lengthy paragraphs usually contain other information that serves to support or explain the major details. Supports for major details are called MINOR DETAILS. While important to overall understanding, minor details are used primarily to add interest or examples to reinforce the more important information. Major details help us to understand a main idea and its relationship to the central theme and topic. To find the major details in a paragraph, ask what information the author has given to help you to understand the message. How has the author supported or explained the main idea? Look again at paragraph 2 from Application 4C, p. 53. Notice how the major details support the main idea.

TOPIC: Collapse of the Confederacy.

MAIN IDEA: In 1864 victories by the Union armies under Sherman and Grant brought about the final collapse of the Confederacy.

MAJOR DETAILS: Sherman took Atlanta and Savannah and devastated Georgia. Grant forced evacuation of Petersburg and Richmond and forced Lee to retreat.

Notice that we've used only the key words from the major support sentences to list the major details. There is no need to copy full sentences from the paragraph. In fact, doing so not only takes too much time but interferes with the process of "weeding out" essential information.

Notice also that you need to identify the topic and main idea of a paragraph in order to find major details. Beware, though, that some sentences in a paragraph may serve a variety of functions. For example, one sentence may introduce the topic *as well as* state the main idea or provide a major support for the main idea. Other sentences may function as introductory, transitional, or concluding statements or may provide further explanation of a major detail. Sometimes long, complex sentences combine these functions.

Example:

Realizing that war would jeopardize national survival, Washington concentrated his attention on diplomacy and military affairs. His reluctance to become involved with pending legislation enabled his energetic secretary of the treasury, Alexander Hamilton, to set the administration's domestic priorities. Hamilton quickly emerged as the country's most imaginative and dynamic statesman by formulating a sweeping program for national economic development. But Hamilton's agenda proved deeply divisive. (p. 208)

TOPIC: Alexander Hamilton and domestic policy under Washington.

MAIN IDEA: Alexander Hamilton, Washington's secretary of the treasury, set the administration's domestic priorities.

MAJOR DETAILS:

Washington concerned with foreign affairs.

Hamilton formulated program for economic development.

Some policies divisive.

EXPLANATION: In this paragraph, the first sentence is introductory; it explains the second sentence's statement that Washington gave control of domestic policy to Hamilton. The second sentence states the topic and main idea of the paragraph. The third sentence describes Hamilton in more detail and adds information that Hamilton's domestic policy focused on national economic development. The last sentence is a transitional sentence that provides the major detail concerning the divisive nature of his policies. This sentence also reveals that subsequent information will not only describe his policies but also explain the problems caused by these policies.

To find major details, sift through the paragraph, looking for the *most important supports for the paragraph's main message.* Don't get sidetracked or lost in the search for important information. Keep in mind that major details are those that directly support the main idea.

APPLICATION 5A: Read the following paragraph. Determine the topic and main idea of the paragraph. Find the major details by identifying information that directly supports the paragraph's main idea. Compare your answers with the suggested responses at the end of Discussion 5.

The U.S. declaration of war in April 1917 found America's military woefully unprepared. The regular army consisted of 120,000 enlisted men, few with combat experience, plus some 80,000 recently federalized National Guardsmen. An aging officer corps dozed away the years until retirement. Enough ammunition was on hand for only two days of fighting. The War Department was a snake pit of jealous bureaucrats, one of whom hoarded twelve thousand typewriters as the war approached. (p. 746)

What are the TOPIC, MAIN IDEA, and MAJOR DETAILS?

> **NOTE:**   The topic, main idea, and major details, when used in this manner, form an *outline* of the author's argument. Notes structured in this way provide an excellent tool for reviewing your textbook. Note also that this paragraph contains other information that explains more about the major details we have listed. These are minor elements. Practice distinguishing major from minor detail. To find the major support information, ask yourself which information is necessary to understanding the author's message.

APPLICATION 5B: Read each paragraph below and identify the topic, main idea, and major details. Compare your responses with the suggested responses at the end of Discussion 5.

Paragraph 1:

The expansion and consolidation of railroading reflected both the ingenuity and the dishonesty flourishing on the corporate-management scene. Although by the 1870s railroads had replaced the patchwork of canal and stagecoach operations that dominated domestic transportation before the Civil War, the industry itself was in a state of chaos. Hundreds of small companies used widely different standards for car couplers, rails, track width, and engine size. Financed by large eastern and British banks, Huntington, Gould, and others devoured these smaller lines to create large, integrated track networks. In the Northeast, four major trunk lines emerged.

In the South four hundred small companies averaging less than forty miles of track apiece were consolidated into five major systems. West of the Mississippi five great lines—the Union Pacific (1869); the Northern Pacific (1883); the Atchison, Topeka, and Santa Fe (1883); the Southern Pacific (1883); and the Great Northern (1893)—controlled most of the track by 1893. (p. 572)

TOPIC: What subject is the paragraph about?

MAIN IDEA: What is the author's message? (Answer the question with a complete sentence.)

MAJOR DETAILS: How does the author support or explain the main idea? Answer using only key words and ideas; do not write long sentences. Try using your own words to phrase your answer.

Paragraph 2:

Collis P. Huntington, Jay Gould, James J. Hill, and the other larger-than-life figures who reorganized and expanded the railroad industry in the 1870s and 1880s were often depicted by their contemporaries as villains and robber barons who manipulated stock markets and company policies to line their own pockets. For example, one competitor scorned Jay Gould, the short, secretive president of the Union Pacific, as a "perfect eel," and newspaper publisher Joseph Pulitzer called him "one of the most sinister figures that have ever flitted batlike across the vision of the American people." Recent historians, however, have pointed out that the great industrialists were a diverse group, and far from all bad. Although some were ironfisted pirates who engaged in deceptive and fraudulent practices, others were upstanding businessmen who managed their companies with sophistication and innovation. Indeed, some of their ideas were breathtaking in their originality and inventiveness. (p. 572).

What are the TOPIC, MAIN IDEA, and MAJOR DETAILS?

Paragraph 3:

Many millions of years after North America's initial separation, during the Mesozoic ("middle life") era—the age of the dinosaurs—violent movements of the earth's crust thrust up the Pacific Coastal, Sierra Nevada, and Cascade ranges on the continent's western edge. As the dinosaurs were dying out, toward the end of the Mesozoic some 65–70 million years ago, the vast, shallow sea that washed over much of west-central North America disappeared, having been replaced by the Rocky Mountains. By then, the decay and fossilization of plant and animal life were creating North America's once great petroleum deposits, which even a generation ago seemed almost limitless. Within the last 50 million years, volcanic eruptions raised the cones that now form the Hawaiian Islands, twenty-five hundred miles southwest of California. Active Pacific-rim volcanoes and powerful earthquakes all over the continent dramatically demonstrate that the molding of the American landscape still continues. (p. xxxvi)

What are the TOPIC, MAIN IDEA, and MAJOR DETAILS?

SUGGESTED RESPONSES to Discussion 5:

Application 5A:

TOPIC: America's military preparedness for World War I

MAIN IDEA: The U.S. declaration of war in April 1917 found America's military woefully unprepared.

MAJOR DETAILS:

Small regular army without combat experience

Aging officer corps

Limited supply of ammunition

War Department run by jealous bureaucrats

Application 5B:

Paragraph 1:

TOPIC: The expansion and consolidation of railroads
(The first sentence introduces the topic.)

MAIN IDEA: (The topic sentence is sentence #4.) Financed by large eastern and British banks, Huntington, Gould, and others devoured smaller lines to create large, integrated track networks.

MAJOR DETAILS: By the 1870s, railroads dominated domestic transportation, but industry was in chaos.

Cause of chaos was hundreds of small companies with lack of compatible parts, tracks, etc.

Huntington, Gould, and others used large eastern and British bank money to buy up small companies and consolidate.

South—five major systems created.

West—five great lines created.

Paragraph 2:

TOPIC: Characteristics of the great industrialists

MAIN IDEA: (The topic sentence is sentence #3.) The great industrialists were a diverse group, and far from all bad.

MAJOR DETAILS: Depicted in their own time as villains and robber barons.

Now thought some were bad, but some were good businessmen who managed companies with sophistication and inventiveness.

Paragraph 3:

TOPIC: Formation of the American landscape

MAIN IDEA: Volcanic eruptions and powerful earthquakes began molding the American landscape during the Mesozoic era and still continue today.

MAJOR DETAILS: Mesozoic ("middle life") era—age of the dinosaurs: Earthquakes formed Western edge mountain ranges.

Toward end of Mesozoic era (65–70 million years ago): Shallow sea disappeared as Rocky Mountains formed.

Petroleum deposits formed from decay and fossilization of plants and animals.

Last 50 million years: Volcanoes formed Hawaiian Islands.

Today: Pacific-rim volcanoes, earthquakes all over continent still active.

DISCUSSION 6: Making Inferences and Assumptions, Evaluating Implications

When a writer suggests an idea but does not put it into words, we say that the writer *implies* the idea. The writer expects the reader to understand that idea just as surely as if it were expressed in print. When a reader grasps an idea that the writer implies, we say that the reader *infers* the idea. While reading, we often have to draw inferences, or "read between the lines." Writers assume that their reader has common background knowledge that allows them to share a message without actually putting it into words.

Making inferences is not as complicated as it may sound. We do it all the time in everyday life, and most of us are very good at it. Consider the following example: When we see a friend crying, we *infer* that something is wrong. We assume so because we all understand that crying usually is related to unhappiness. We also know that people sometimes cry when they are happy, but this behavior is usually accompanied by other signs, such as smiling or laughing. If our friend does not show these other signs, our first assumption is that something is wrong. In making inferences, we look for clues to verify our assumptions. Making inferences entails drawing conclusions or formulating hypotheses based on something that is understood but not said. Once we draw an inference, we analyze evidence either to verify or to discard our original hypothesis.

Another example of how we grasp implications might be helpful. If a friend says, "My candidate won the race," we can infer that he or she is talking about an election, not a horse race. We would make this inference based on our knowledge of the usual meaning of the word *candidate*. If our friend had earlier mentioned the 1992 presidential race, we could also infer that Clinton was the candidate whom he or she supported. Even though it was not actually said, we can assume so because of the wording of the sentence and the background information we have. Inferences are assumptions, or suppositions, that we make based on the evidence at hand. Consider the following:

The old delight in hacking enemies' corpses in the public square and exposing their heads on palings went out of fashion—gradually and with conspicuous exceptions such as the displays made of sachem Philip and "squaw sachem" Weetamoo in "King Philip's War." (Jennings, p. 163)

The writer does not expressly say that King Philip's and Weetamoo's heads were displayed in public, but he *implies* it. We are expected to *infer* that this happened. We assume that the author intends us to draw this conclusion.

Readers must use careful judgment when making inferences. To make appropriate inferences, look for any idea or information that the author might assume you will understand even though he or she does not expressly state the idea. Ask yourself whether the author is suggesting an idea rather than actually saying it.

Be careful not to go too far when making inferences. We all know people who "jump" to conclusions or who make inferences too quickly. Take care to draw only those conclusions suggested by the author.

Making inferences is essential to reading for meaning. In fact, you used this skill in Discussion 4 to identify unstated main ideas. You use inferences to read actively, to evaluate the material critically. To analyze an author's message, you need to identify the assumptions and conclusions that the author states or implies. Critical readers try to detect the assumptions underlying the author's message and weigh the author's implications and conclusions.

APPLICATION 6:   Read the following paragraph again from Discussion 5. The topic, main idea, and major details are identified below the paragraph. To hone your skill in making inferences, ask yourself these questions:

1. Does the author expect me to understand more about the main idea that is expressly stated?

2. If so, what kind of background knowledge does the author assume I have about the main idea?

3. What conclusions does the author intend me to reach?

Compare your responses with the suggested responses at the end of Discussion 6.

The expansion and consolidation of railroading reflected both the ingenuity and the dishonesty flourishing on the corporate-management scene. Although by the 1870s railroads had replaced the patchwork of canal and stagecoach operations that dominated domestic transportation before the Civil War, the industry itself was in a state of chaos. Hundreds of small companies used widely different standards for car couplers, rails, track width, and engine size. Financed by large eastern and British banks, Huntington, Gould, and others devoured these smaller lines to create large, integrated track networks. In the Northeast, four major trunk lines emerged. In the South four hundred small companies averaging less than forty miles of track apiece were consolidated into five major systems. West of the Mississippi five great lines—the Union Pacific (1969); the Northern Pacific (1883); the Atchison, Topeka, and Santa Fe (1883); the Southern Pacific (1883); and the Great Northern (1893)—controlled most of the track by 1893. (p. 572)

TOPIC: The expansion and consolidation of railroads

MAIN IDEA: Financed by large eastern and British banks, Huntington, Gould, and others devoured smaller rail lines to create large, integrated track networks.

MAJOR DETAILS: By the 1870s, railroads dominated domestic transportation, but industry was in chaos.

Cause of chaos was hundreds of small companies with lack of compatible parts, tracks, etc.

Huntington, Gould, and others used large eastern and British bank money to buy up small companies and consolidate.

South—five major systems created.

West—five great lines created.

What are your INFERENCES?

Evaluating Implications

An author's assumptions may be implied intentionally or unintentionally. At times an author may be unaware that his or her interpretations are biased and that they therefore "slant" the information. Sometimes an author may omit essential information or use implication to mislead the reader purposely.

In Part II, Discussion 3, you saw that frame of reference, point of view, and use of fact and opinion reflect authors' interpretations, assumptions, and conclusions and may shape readers' perceptions of meaning. Part II, Discussion 5, examined authors' purpose and tone, and stressed the need to recognize these qualities while determining authors' underlying messages. All of these elements affect authors' implications and readers' inferences. When you make inferences, try to determine whether the author presents, in an unbiased manner, all information essential for supporting his or her assumptions and conclusions.

You are familiar with biased implications used in advertising and political campaigns. We can also find biased implications in news reporting. Consider the following: "The president refused to answer questions from the press and would not admit to having access to current information concerning the new development in this administration's latest of many scandals. . . ." Here we see how the wording of a message reflects biased, negative implications. The author of this statement expects the reader to infer that some wrongdoing is being "covered up" and that such tactics are normal in the administration. An unbiased account of the same information would be neither positive nor negative and might read as follows: "The president said that he would not comment on the new development until he met with his advisers and had a chance to check the accuracy of the information. . . ." Here the information is presented in a straightforward manner. The wording carries very little implication based on assumption. The only inferences needed are those natural to common knowledge of our language. For example, we share a common understanding of *president* and *advisers* that, based on previous context, would allow us to assume *which* president and *which* advisers are being discussed in the article. This is normal inference expected of a reader.

Well-known college textbooks are carefully edited and reviewed to eliminate biased wording and implication by omission. However, readers must be aware that all authors' assumptions, interpretations, and conclusions need to be analyzed for implied meaning. Be ready to determine whether authors' implications appear intentional or unintentional.

Inferential reading is such a basic element of all thinking, writing, reading, speaking, and listening that it is impossible to separate it out as a "skill" to be studied. Examining authors' implications and assumptions, making inferences, and drawing conclusions are natural processes that we all develop with awareness and practice. Experienced readers search consciously for meaning beyond the words printed on a page. They ask questions for additional meaning as they read. They ask not only, "What does the author say?" but also, "What does the author mean?"

For two excellent resources on the critical thinking and questioning processes described here, consult John Chaffee's *Thinking Critically* and Neil Brown and Stuart Keely's *Asking the Right Questions.*

SUGGESTED RESPONSES to Discussion 6:

Application 6:

In the paragraph's first sentence, the author uses the word *dishonesty*. The author does so to suggest (imply) that some corporate managers responsible for takeovers of smaller companies used illegal means. The paragraph does not identify these "dishonest" practices, but we assume that the author intends us to keep the idea of dishonesty in mind as we read about the "ingenious" takeovers. We can confirm this assumption by noticing the use of the words *devoured these smaller lines.* By employing this phrasing, the author implies—and the reader infers—that these corporate people proved ruthless in putting small companies out of business.

DISCUSSION 7: Determining Organizational Patterns in Paragraphs

In well-written paragraphs, ideas and information follow certain patterns. Experienced readers use these patterns to understand the author's message, to identify major details, and to determine the relationships between the major details and the paragraph's main idea. In Part II, we discussed the need to know the "why" of history and relationships among historical events. Understanding organizational patterns is a key to understanding relationships. This in turn helps us to perceive the broad picture, the "why" of history that you are expected to understand as you work through your course.

There are many types of paragraph patterns; only a few of the most common appear below. The patterns of organization most often used by textbook authors are:

Sequence/Time Order

Cause/Effect

Comparison/Contrast

Definition

Description

Listing/Example

Most complex paragraphs contain more than one organizational pattern. However, in such cases, one of these patterns usually predominates. Authors often use "signal clues" to help their readers to follow the patterns. These clues are words that hint at the pattern used in the paragraph. Read the explanations and examples below. Each represents a particular paragraph pattern found in *The Enduring Vision,* 3rd ed.

Time Order/Sequence Pattern

The time order (chronological order) pattern relies on the sequence of events. Such a paragraph pattern shows *when* events occurred in relation to each other. Authors use signal words such as *after, before, when, then,* and *until* to guide you through the sequence of events. Sometimes a series of dates signal sequence, but this is not always true. When dates are given, they may be mixed with other patterns such as cause/effect.

Other sequence patterns show steps in a process or order of importance. The sequence pattern used in the exercises in this guide is based on the time order/sequence pattern because it is the one most often used in your history text.

Example:

About 10,000 B.C. the Ice Age was nearing its end. Melting glaciers had opened up an ice-free corridor leading from Alaska to the northern Plains. Bands of hunters moved through this corridor, and others probably traveled south along the Pacific coast by boat. As they emerged from the glacier-covered north, they discovered a hunter's paradise. Giant mammoths, mastodons, horses, camels, bison, caribou, and moose, as well as smaller species roamed the continent innocent of the ways of human predators. So bountiful and accommodating was this new environment that the Paleo-Indians, as archaeologists call these hunters, fanned out and proliferated with astonishing speed. By 9000 B.C. descendants of the first Americans had dispersed throughout the Western Hemisphere. (p. 2)

TOPIC: The discovery and settlement of the Western Hemisphere

MAIN IDEA: Paleo-Indians moved through the Alaska corridor and settled the Western Hemisphere about 10,000 to 9,000 B.C.

MAJOR DETAILS: About 10,000 B.C. melting glaciers left ice-free corridor from Alaska to Western Hemisphere.

Bands of hunters called Paleo-Indians moved through corridor and/or traveled by boat down Pacific coast.

Discovered good hunting grounds.

By 9000 B.C. had settled throughout Western Hemisphere.

EXPLANATION: This paragraph uses a sequence pattern because it relates events that occurred during a specific time period. The series of events happened in order, one after another. Signal clues are dates.

Cause/Effect Pattern

Cause/effect (cause/result) patterns show how events or developments result from or affect each other. A paragraph that uses this pattern presents the reasons why something happened and the effects that it had. Some common signal words for the cause/effect pattern are *because, resulted from, as a result of, consequently,* and *therefore.* Numerous signals exist for this kind of pattern, many of which may require inferences. (See Part III, Discussion 6.)

Example:

The warming of the earth's atmosphere continued until about 4000 B.C., with far-reaching effects on the North American content. Sea levels rose, flooding shallow areas, and glacial runoff in the interior filled the Great Lakes, the Mississippi River basin, and other waterways. As the glaciers receded northward, so did the arctic and subarctic environments that had previously extended far into what are now the "lower 48" states of the United States. Treeless plains and evergreen forests gave way to deciduous forests in the East, grassland prairies on the Plains, and desert in much of the West. An immense range of flora and fauna, both on land and in the waters, came to characterize the American landscape. We are familiar with many of these same plants and animals today. (p. 3)

TOPIC: The effects of warming of the earth's atmosphere on the North American continent

MAIN IDEA: The warming of the earth's atmosphere had far-reaching effects on the North American continent. (Sentence #1 is the topic sentence.)

MAJOR DETAILS: Sea levels rose, flooding shallow areas.

Glacial runoff filled Great Lakes and waterways.

Arctic and subarctic climates receded

Deciduous forests in East formed.

Grassland prairies on plains formed.

Desert in West formed.

Immense range of flora and fauna developed.

EXPLANATION: The first sentence in this paragraph is a good example of a topic sentence. The author signals the cause/effect pattern by telling us that the paragraph discusses the effects of the warming of the continent. These effects serve as the major details of the paragraph.

Comparison/Contrast Pattern

Comparison/contrast patterns show how objects, people, events, or developments are alike or different. A comparison pattern shows likenesses; a contrast pattern shows differences.

Some paragraphs show only comparison; they tell only how things resemble each other. Common signal words for the comparison pattern are *just as, as, like,* and *the same as*. Other paragraphs show only contrast; they tell only how things are different. Common signal words for the contrast pattern are *however, but, different from, than, in contrast to,* and *yet*.

Some paragraphs mix both comparison and contrast. This mixed approach is probably the most common.

Example:

Although both sides engaged in mudslinging, Jackson's men had better aim. Charges by Adams's supporters that Jackson was an illiterate backwoodsman only added to Jackson's popular appeal by making him seem just like an ordinary citizen. Jackson's supporters portrayed the clash as one between "the *democracy* of the *country,* on the one hand, and a *lordly purse-proud aristocracy* on the other." Jackson, they said, was the common man incarnate—his mind unclouded by learning, his morals simple and true, his will fierce and resolute. In contrast, Jackson's men represented Adams as an aristocrat, a dry scholar whose learning obscured the truth, a man who could write but not fight. Much of this, of course, was wild exaggeration. Jackson was a wealthy planter, not a simple backwoodsman. But it was what people wanted to hear. Uncorrupt, natural, plain, Jackson was presented as the common man's image of his better self. (pp. 303–304)

TOPIC: Mudslinging by Jackson's and Adams's supporters in 1828 election

MAIN IDEA: Jackson benefited from the mudslinging campaign conducted by both parties in the 1828 election.

MAJOR DETAILS: Jackson called illiterate backwoodsman.

Adams called an aristocrat and dry scholar, afraid to fight.

Jackson portrayed as "common man."

Jackson really a wealthy planter.

Jackson portrayed as uncorrupt, natural, plain.

EXPLANATION: This paragraph compares and contrasts the claims made by supporters of each candidate. The primary pattern is contrast. Signal clues are *although, both, in contrast, but*. The first sentence is the topic sentence and contains the main idea.

Definition Pattern

The definition pattern presents an idea or term and then defines, explains, or describes it in the paragraph. Signal words may or may not be present. The paragraph may introduce the pattern with a simple *is* or *this means*. Many times, readers must infer this pattern.

Example:

What was progressivism? On a few points, all students of the movement agree. First, it was a political response to industrialization and its social by-products: immigration, urban growth, the concentration of corporate power, and the widening of class divisions. Second, it was in most cases distinct from populism, the reform movement that preceded it. Whereas populism attracted aggrieved farmers, progressivism's strength lay in the cities. Progressivism enlisted far more journalists, academics, and social theorists than did populism. Finally, the progressives were *reformers*, not radicals or revolutionaries. They wanted to remedy the social evils spawned by capitalism, not destroy the system itself. (p. 707)

TOPIC: Definition of progressivism

> **MAIN IDEA:**   Progressivism was a political response to industrialization and its social by-products and differed from the populist movement.

>> **MAJOR DETAILS:**   Political response to: immigration, urban growth, corporate power, class division issues.
>>
>> Differed from populist movement—attracted city people and scholars.
>>
>> Reformers, not revolutionaries.

EXPLANATION: This paragraph explains the term *progressivism* as it applied to a political movement. The idea of progressivism is defined by description and by contrast with another movement. This paragraph uses a mixed pattern of definition and comparison/contrast.

Description Pattern

An author chooses this pattern to describe an idea, person, setting, or event in detail. Sensory imagery is used to help readers visualize what is being described. The author may or may not use signal clues, and the reader usually has to infer this pattern.

Example:

Western North America's "backbone" is the Rocky Mountains. In turn, the Rockies form part of the immense mountain system that reaches from Alaska to the Andes of South America. Elevations in the Rockies rise from a mile above sea level at Denver at the foot of the mountains to permanently snowcapped peaks more than fourteen thousand feet above sea level. Beyond the front range of the Rockies lies the Continental Divide, the watershed separating the rivers flowing eastward into the Atlantic from those draining westward into the Pacific. The climate and vegetation of the Rocky Mountain high country resemble Arctic and subarctic types. (p. xxxviii)

TOPIC: The Rocky Mountains

> **MAIN IDEA:**   The Rocky Mountains form the "backbone" of western North America.

>> **MAJOR DETAILS:**   Description of Rockies:
>>
>> Part of mountain range that extends from Alaska to Andes of South America.
>>
>> Height of one mile above sea level at Denver to 14,000 feet above sea level.
>>
>> Continental Divide separates rivers flowing east and west.
>>
>> Arctic and subarctic climate and vegetation.

EXPLANATION: This paragraph gives information about the location, height, climate, vegetation, and importance of the Rocky Mountain range as the Continental Divide.

Listing/Example Pattern

In the listing pattern, the author presents examples or details of equal importance. In other words, the author could arrange the details in any order, and the paragraph's meaning would stay the same. This pattern is sometimes called the "example" pattern or the "addition" pattern. Many signal words exist; the most common include *also, for example, in addition to,* and *for instance.*

Example:

In addition to large-scale transformations in production, transportation, and income, the two decades before the Civil War witnessed subtle alterations in the quality of everyday life in the United States. Less visible and dramatic than those wrought by the railroad, these changes in everyday experiences occurred for the most part within the privacy of homes and affected such routine activities as eating, drinking, and washing. Technological improvements in these years made the daily home-life experiences of Americans far more comfortable. "Think of the numberless contrivances and inventions for our comfort and luxury which the last half dozen years have brought forth," the poet Walt Whitman exclaimed to his readers, and you will "bless your star that fate has cast your lot in the year of Our Lord 1857." Indeed, the patent office in Washington was flooded with sketches of reclining seats, sliding tables, beds convertible into chairs, lounges convertible into cradles, street-sweeping machines, and fly traps. Machine-made furniture began to transform the interiors of houses. Stoves revolutionized heating and cooking. By bringing fresh vegetables to city dwellers, railroads stimulated important changes in diet. (p. 340)

TOPIC: Technological improvements for everyday life.

MAIN IDEA: Technological improvements enhanced the quality of daily home life for many Americans in the two decades before the Civil War.

MAJOR DETAILS: Daily life made more comfortable.

Many inventions created to improve home.

Machine-made furniture.

Stoves revolutionized heating and cooking.

Railroads brought vegetables to city and contributed to change in diet.

EXPLANATION: This paragraph gives examples of the improvements in home life as a result of technological advances in the 1840s and 1850s. The examples do not need to be presented in any particular order. The paragraph also uses a cause/effect pattern; note that the examples listed are the *result* of technological invention. The listing pattern is often mixed with other patterns, especially in history textbooks.

APPLICATION 7: In each paragraph below, determine which of the six organizational patterns predominates. If the pattern is mixed, decide which pattern most strongly influences the overall meaning of the paragraph. To find the pattern of organization, ask yourself how the author has organized the material to show the relationships between the main idea and major details. Compare your answers to the suggested responses shown at the end of the set of paragraphs.

Paragraph 1:

Regardless of which path a politician chose, all leaders in the 1820s and 1830s had to adapt to the rising democratic idea of politics as a forum for the expression of the will of the common people rather than as an activity that gentlemen conducted for the people. Gentlemen could still be elected to office, but their success now depended less on their education or wealth than on their ability to identify and follow the will of the majority. Americans still looked up to their political leaders, but the leaders could no longer look down on the people. (p. 300)

Pattern of organization?

Paragraph 2:

Outside the South factory owners turned to unskilled immigrant laborers for the muscle needed in the booming factories, mills, railroads, and heavy-construction industries. In Philadelphia, where native-born Americans and recent German immigrants dominated the highly skilled metal-working trades, Irish newcomers remained mired in unskilled horsecarting and construction occupations until the 1890s, when the "new immigrants" from southern and eastern Europe replaced them (see Chapter 19). In the Northeast poverty-stricken French-Canadians filled the most menial positions in the textile mills. On the West Coast Chinese immigrants performed the dirtiest and most physically demanding jobs in mining, canning, and railroad construction. (p. 589)

Pattern of organization?

Paragraph 3:

As early as 1826, an American "empresario," Haden Edwards, led a revolt against Mexican rule, but Mexican forces, aided by Stephen F. Austin, quickly crushed the uprising. Although, like Austin, most Americans were still willing to live in Texas as naturalized Mexican citizens, during the early 1830s, the allegiance of the Americans to the Mexican government was severely eroded. In 1830 Mexico closed Texas to further immigration from the United States and, having emancipated its own slaves in 1829, forbade the introduction of more slaves into Texas. The latter measure struck directly at the Americans, many of whom were slaveholders. However, Mexico lacked the military might to enforce its decrees. Between 1830 and 1834, the number of Americans in Texas doubled. In 1834 Austin secured repeal of the 1830 prohibition on American immigration, and by 1835 an estimated one thousand Americans a month were crossing into Texas. In 1836 Texas contained some 30,000 white Americans, 5,000 black slaves, and 4,000 Mexicans. (p. 411)

Pattern of organization?

Paragraph 4:

Even as Polk was challenging Britain over Oregon, the United States and Mexico moved steadily toward war. The impending conflict had both remote and immediate causes. One long-standing grievance lay in the failure of the Mexican government to pay some $2 million in debts owed to American citizens. In addition, bitter memories of the Alamo and of the Goliad massacre continued to arouse in Americans a loathing of Mexicans. Above all, the issue of Texas embroiled relations between the two nations. Mexico still hoped to regain Texas or at least to keep it independent of the United States. Once in control of Texas, the Mexicans feared, the United States might seize other Mexican provinces, perhaps even Mexico itself, and treat the citizens of Mexico much as it had treated its slaves. (p. 419)

Pattern of organization?

Paragraph 5:

Van Buren exemplified a new breed of politician. A tavernkeeper's son, he had started his political career in county politics and worked his way up to New York's governorship. In Albany he built a powerful political machine, the Albany Regency, composed mainly of men like himself from the lower and middling ranks. His arch rival in New York politics, DeWitt Clinton, was all that Van Buren was not—tall, handsome, aristocratic, and brilliant. But Van Buren had a geniality that made ordinary people feel comfortable and an uncanny ability to sense in which direction the political winds were about to blow. Van Buren loved politics, which he viewed as a wonderful game; he was one of the first prominent American politicians to make personal friends from among his political enemies. (p. 303)

Pattern of organization?

Paragraph patterns and relationships are easier to understand than they might seem. Almost everyone has practiced using patterns of organization while writing paragraphs and essays in English classes. As a reader, identifying organization patterns in paragraphs and longer passages provides a tremendous tool for distilling meaning. It is especially valuable for understanding long, complicated, highly detailed paragraphs. Once you recognize such patterns, the main ideas and major details often fall into place.

> **NOTE:**   When taking textbook or class notes, record the information by following the same pattern used by the book or instructor. This technique comes in very handy when reviewing for a test (especially an essay exam), for you will need to understand the relationships within the material under study. Remember: it is not enough to memorize the "what" and "how" of historical data. You need to delve deeper and to be able to explain concepts and relationships during class discussions and tests. Understanding relationships among broad concepts is a basic part of thinking critically about the "why" of history.

SUGGESTED RESPONSES to Discussion 7:

Application 7:

Paragraph 1: Comparison/Contrast

EXPLANATION: The comparison/contrast pattern is clear in this paragraph, for the author discusses such matters as politics *by* the people instead of *for* the people; politicians' education and wealth as less important than the ability to represent will of the majority; leaders' inability to look down on people. Signal words are *rather than, less, than, still, but, no longer.*

Paragraph 2: Listing/Example

EXPLANATION: The topic of this paragraph is the employment of unskilled immigrant labor in industry. The first sentence is a good example of a topic sentence that contains the paragraph's main idea. The major details are listed as examples of the kinds of unskilled labor used. The order in which the author presents these details makes no difference to meaning. There are *no* signal words used in this paragraph; you must infer the pattern from the major details.

Paragraph 3: Primarily Sequence/Time Order, with Cause/Effect secondary

EXPLANATION: The topic of this paragraph is the erosion of allegiance to the Mexican government on the part of American settlers in Texas. The second sentence is the topic sentence, containing the main idea of the paragraph. The signal for the sequence pattern is the topic sentence's reference to the early 1830s. Major details follow, presented in sequential order of the events described. The paragraph also uses a pattern of cause/effect, but the sequence pattern predominates.

Paragraph 4: Primarily Cause/Effect, with Listing secondary

EXPLANATION: The topic for this paragraph is the factors that led the United States and Mexico to war. The main idea appears in the second sentence: "The impending conflict had both remote and immediate *causes.*" Here the author tells the reader that the pattern is cause/effect. The reader can then anticipate that the paragraph's major details will be causes and/or results. Here the causes and effects are listed, and the listing pattern is signaled by such words as *one, in addition,* and *above all.*

Paragraph 5: Primarily Description/Definition Mixed, with Definition secondary

EXPLANATION: The topic of this paragraph is Van Buren. The first sentence is a topic sentence and signals both description *and* definition. The reader anticipates that the remainder of this paragraph will focus on Van Buren as a new breed of politician, and that the author will define "new breed of politician." The main signal clue here is the word *exemplified*.

DISCUSSION 8: Analyzing Difficult Text: The "Journalists' Questions"

So far, you have worked on identifying central themes, topics, main ideas, major details, and organization patterns. Armed with these skills, you should be able to extract the most important information from your textbook. However, some passages and paragraphs are so complex or so packed with ideas and details that you may need to dig deeper to understand them. A system for double-checking your comprehension will come in handy.

For information-loaded text and difficult-to-read passages, try asking what are sometimes called "journalists' questions." These are the *what, where, when, why,* and *how* queries that writers use to develop information. You don't need to use this method for everything you read; only for the hard-to-understand material. This method requires frequent stopping, questioning, and summarizing, and it demands total interaction with the reading matter.

Before using "journalists' questions," always read the paragraph first and identify the topic, main idea, and the pattern of organization (See Application 8A). Then analyze the sentences in the paragraph one at a time by using the questioning technique in Application 8B. Use the information in the sentences as clues to which questions you should ask; your questions should "grow" out of the text material itself.

APPLICATION 8A: Skim the paragraph below to get an idea of what it's about and how it is organized.

The railroads' vicious competition did not abate until a national depression that began in 1893 forced a number of roads into the hands of the investment bankers on whom they had become increasingly dependent. Supported by the major investment houses in Boston, New York, and Philadelphia, J. Pierpont Morgan, a massively built man with piercing eyes and a commanding presence, took over the weakened systems, reorganized their administration, refinanced their debts, and built intersystem alliances by purchasing substantial blocks of stock in the competing roads. By 1906, thanks to the bankers' centralized management, seven giant networks controlled two-thirds of the nation's rail mileage. (p. 573)

Answer the following questions. Compare your responses with the suggested responses that follow Discussion 8.

1. What is the paragraph topic?

2. What is the paragraph's main idea?

3. What pattern of organization is used?

APPLICATION 8B: Now you are ready to question the details. The first step in analyzing highly detailed information is to read the material carefully while questioning constantly.

The paragraph from Application 8A is repeated below. In parentheses following each sentence are the kinds of "journalists' questions" you should ask yourself. Answer them and then check your answers with the suggested responses.

The railroads' vicious competition did not abate until a national depression that began in 1893 forced a number of roads into the hands of the investment bankers on whom they had become increasingly dependent. (1. What brought an end to the railroad's vicious competition?) (2. When did this happen?) (3. Why did the roads go to the bankers?) Supported by the major investment houses in Boston, New York, and Philadelphia, J. Pierpont Morgan, a massively built man with piercing eyes and a commanding presence, took over the weakened systems, reorganized their administration, refinanced their debts, and built intersystem alliances by purchasing substantial blocks of stock in the competing roads. (4. Who took over the railroads?) (5. How was he able to do this?) (6. What changes did he make?) (7. How were intersystem alliances formed?) By 1906, thanks to the bankers' centralized management, seven giant networks controlled two-thirds of the nation's rail mileage. (8. How many giant networks were formed?) (9. How much rail mileage did they control?) (10. What accounted for this success?) (11. When was this accomplished?).

As you use this method to understand difficult passages in your textbook, you will probably find it most valuable for reading paragraphs that have unstated main ideas and/or those that require you to make many inferences. While sorting through the information, try to determine which information is most important and which is least important. To rank information in this way, use the topic, main idea, or the pattern of organization.

Analyzing, Paraphrasing, and Summarizing

When you have finished using "journalists' questions" to analyze a paragraph or passage, look back over the information that you have written. If you have asked the right questions, your answers will form the key elements for a summary of the material. Try to summarize the information in your own words. Such paraphrasing and summarizing is an excellent way to check how well you understand the author's message and major details.

APPLICATION 8C: Now you are ready to write a summary *in your own words*. Start by looking at your answers to Application 8B. Begin your summary with a sentence that states the paragraph's topic and main idea. Then use the information from your questions. As you write your summary, follow the same pattern of organization that the authors used in the original text. Check your summary against the one shown in the suggested response.

> **NOTE:**   You can use this same system to summarize a long passage, an entire section of text, or a whole chapter. To summarize long, detailed passages, determine the key elements such as central themes, main

ideas, and patterns of organization. List the key elements; then use your own words to create sentences incorporating the most important ideas and relationships. For chapter summaries, write a paragraph stating the main concepts and combining central themes for each section of text. Include only elements related to the overall message of the section. Remember that a summary is like a snapshot; focus only on the main subject.

SUGGESTED RESPONSES to Discussion 8:

Application 8A:

1. TOPIC: Reorganization of railroads 1893–1906

2. MAIN IDEA: J. P. Morgan consolidated railroads and built intersystem alliances to form giant networks after many companies went bankrupt during the depression.

3. PATTERN OF ORGANIZATION: Cause/Effect and Sequence

Application 8B:

1. *What brought an end to the railroad's vicious competition?* Banks took control.

2. *When did this happen?* 1893

3. *Why did the roads go to the bankers?* National depression forced owners in debt to lose railroads.

4. *Who took over the railroads?* J. P. Morgan

5. *How was he able to do this?* He was supported by eastern investment houses.

6. *What changes did he make?* He reorganized administration, refinanced debts, and built intersystem alliances.

7. *How were intersystem alliances formed?* Large blocks of stocks in competing roads were bought.

8. *How many giant networks were formed?* Seven giant networks were formed.

9. *How much rail mileage did they control?* They controlled two-thirds of the nation's rail mileage.

10. *What accounted for this success?* Success was due to bankers' centralized management.

11. *When was this accomplished?* This was accomplished by 1906.

Application 8C:

Banks took control of many competing railroads in 1893 during the depression. J. P. Morgan, supported by eastern investment houses, took control, reorganized administration, refinanced debts, built intersystem alliances, and bought large blocks of stocks in competing roads. Seven giant networks were formed that controlled two-thirds of the nation's rail mileage. The success of this undertaking was due to the bankers' centralized management and was accomplished by 1906.

DISCUSSION 9: Reviewing and Studying Your History Text: Preparing for Exams

You are well on your way to mastering the techniques for reviewing and studying your history textbook. Many valuable books about study techniques are available in libraries and bookstores. However, be aware that all study-skill methods are based on the assumption that you have critically read the material required in your course *before* you begin to review and study. *Critical thinking and reading come first.* There are no shortcuts. Study-skill training can help only if you have first read the material and prepared your notes properly.

Taking Notes While Reading

Below are tips for taking notes as you read. These are general guidelines only; there is no one "right" way to take notes, but some kinds of notetaking can be more effective than others. Over time, you will develop your own style based on what helps you the most. Try these suggestions to see what works for you.

1. Read a passage or several paragraphs all the way through. *Do not stop to take notes or underline your text.* State the central theme in your own words and then write it in the margin of the text. If you do not want to mark your textbook, or if the margins do not provide enough space, use a separate sheet of paper, fold it in half, and line it up with the column you are reading. Be sure to record the page number and column number at the top of the sheet.

2. Go back to the beginning of the passage and take it apart paragraph by paragraph. For each paragraph, identify the topic and the main idea. Write these in the margin or on your notepaper column.

3. Determine the patterns of organization the author has used in developing the passage. Note them in the margin or on your paper.

4. Determine the main idea and *major* details of each of the passage's paragraphs, and list them in the margin or on your paper, using the key words only. Don't write more than you have to.

If you underline, do so sparingly and only *after* you have determined the topic, main idea, and major details. That way, you will underline only the most important information. Underlining without first understanding the main elements will prompt you to mark everything and will do more harm than good. Besides, when you review later, you will have to reread everything you underlined, and you'll be back where you started. Use underlining sensibly. Also, write your notes and underline in *pencil,* not ink. That way, you can change them if necessary.

Do not highlight your textbook. As shocking as this may sound, highlighting your textbook while taking notes interferes with your reviewing the material. It is distracting to see bright colors on the page. Indeed, reading researchers call this kind of distraction "noise." The highlighted sections will draw your attention away from critical information in the text. When you have finished reviewing your notes and text, you might highlight key concepts as a final comprehension check, but do so only after you have constructed your notes and studied them.

5. If the paragraph is long, complicated, and full of details, use the "journalists'" method shown in Discussion 8 for questioning sentence by sentence. Make notes in the text margin or in your notepaper column as you answer your questions.

Using these methods to develop passage-by-passage marginal notes as you read will provide you with a valuable informal outline in the margin of your text. It may take time to put the notes there, but the method will save you hours when you review, for you will be focusing on the essential information.

> **NOTE:** If you use separate paper instead of the text margins, open your textbook to the matching pages in your notes as you review. That way, you can look up anything questionable in your notes. Also, keep your notes conveniently next to the text columns when you attend class. Open your book to the sections under discussion, and add to your notes any related information presented in class. Use a different color of pencil or pen to add class notes so that you can later distinguish between the two. You will be surprised by how quickly you will be able to take efficient and effective notes.

Reviewing Your Notes: Paraphrasing

When you are ready to review, look over your notes and summarize the information. If you used your own words (paraphrased) as you wrote your notes, this step will be easy. Your notes should contain the author's key words and information intermingled with your own words. Bring these words together in sentences while looking at your notes. Then cover your notes, and review those sentences either out loud or in your mind. (It's okay to talk to yourself while you review; college students do so all the time!) If you don't understand your notes, or if you have trouble remembering the information, go back to the paragraph and read it again. Paraphrasing while reviewing works wonderfully for checking your comprehension and recall before exams.

The beauty of this system is that you don't have to rely on someone else to help you study. You also will know what you do and do not understand. Besides, it's much better than the alternative—staring at three hundred pages of underlined or highlighted print.

Preparing for Exams

Surprisingly, there is no mystery to how professors create test questions. They do so by thinking through the material in the textbook and class lectures and discussions with the same questioning techniques presented throughout this book. Their test questions "grow" from the material and focus on ideas, relationships, and patterns. Professors don't want to trick you with complicated question formats; they are looking for responses that show that you have used critical thinking to understand the subject.

The study and review suggestions below will help you to prepare for any kind of exam (even essay exams). Success on exams hinges on reading the material and taking notes that focus on paraphrasing *key concepts* and *relationships* rather than memorizing text word-for-word. Mastering the details is easy once you fit them into the conceptual framework. When you read and review, question the messages of the authors and professor. Think critically about the information you are paraphrasing and summarizing so that when you face the test, you will be able to respond regardless of how the questions are worded. This critical thinking is most essential when preparing for essay exams, for these tests require you to answer in your own words. Learning to paraphrase and summarize as you study will encourage you to think through and analyze ideas and evidence rather than to memorize words, and exams will seem far less frightening.

APPLICATION 9A: This exercise asks you to read a five-paragraph passage, "The Character of Industrial Change." Read the entire passage for central theme. Compare your response with the suggested response on p. 82.

THE CHARACTER OF INDUSTRIAL CHANGE

Five features dominated the birth of modern industrial America after the Civil War: first, the exploitation of immense coal deposits as a source of cheap energy; second, the rapid spread of technological innovation and the factory system; third, the constant pressure on firms to compete tooth-and-nail by cutting costs and prices— as well the impulse to eliminate rivals and create monopolies; fourth, the relentless drop in price levels (a stark contrast to the inflation of other eras); and finally, the failure of the money supply to keep pace with productivity, a development that drove up interest rates and restricted the availability of credit.

All five factors were closely related. The great bituminous coal deposits in Pennsylvania, West Virginia, and Kentucky provided the cheap energy that fueled the railroads, the factories, and explosive urban growth. Exploiting these inexpensive energy sources, new technologies stimulated productivity and catalyzed breathtaking industrial expansion. Technology also enabled manufacturers to cut costs and hire cheap unskilled or semi-skilled labor. This cost cutting in turn drove firms to undersell each other, destroying weaker competitors and prompting stronger, more efficient (and more ruthless) ones to consolidate. At least until the mid-1890s, cost reduction, new technology, and fierce competition forced down overall price levels. Farmers and industrial workers suffered from chronically low agricultural commodity prices and wages, but in their capacity as consumers, they (and all Americans) benefited as store-bought goods cheapened. Meanwhile, high interest rates and the difficulty of obtaining credit added to the burdens of farmers and small entrepreneurs. And almost everyone suffered terribly during the depression years, when the government did nothing to relieve distress. "The sufferings of the working classes are daily increasing," wrote one Philadelphia worker in 1874. "Famine has broken into the home of many of us, and is at the door of all." Above all, business leaders' unflagging drive to maximize efficiency both created colossal fortunes at the top of the economic ladder and forced millions of wage earners to live near the subsistence level.

Out of the new industrial system poured dismal clouds of haze and soot—as well as the first tantalizing trickle of what would become an avalanche of consumer goods. In turn, mounting demands for consumer goods stimulated heavy industry's production of "capital goods"—machines to boost farm and factory output. Together with the railroads, the corporations that manufactured capital goods, refined petroleum, and made steel became the driving force in the nation's economic growth.

A stunning expansion in the *scale* of industry offered tangible evidence of the magnitude of economic change. By the turn of the century, mammoth corporations dominated industrial production. The Singer Sewing Machine Company, for example, with capitalization (operating capital) of $20 million in 1905, boasted eight factories and more than 90,000 employees who made and sold 1.25 million sewing machines annually. Huge companies similarly achieved marvels of production in the railroad, meatpacking, steel, sugar, and oil industries.

Competition among the aggressive and innovative capitalists who headed American heavy industry was intense— and as the post-Civil War era opened, nowhere was it more intense than among the nation's railroads, which to many Americans most symbolized industrial progress. (pp. 570–571)

Write the central theme in your own words.

APPLICATION 9B: The paragraphs of "The Character of Industrial Change" are repeated separately below. For each paragraph, write marginal notes. Remember that there is more than one "right" way to develop notes from text; the important thing is to emphasize key concepts, supports, and relationships. These provide the conceptual framework necessary to understanding, remembering, and applying what you learn from your reading. Compare your responses with the suggested responses.

Paragraph 1:

THE CHARACTER OF INDUSTRIAL CHANGE

Five features dominated the birth of modern industrial America after the Civil War: first, the exploitation of immense coal deposits as a source of cheap energy; second, the rapid spread of technological innovation and the factory system; third, the constant pressure on firms to compete tooth and nail by cutting costs and prices, as well as the impulse to eliminate rivals and create monopolies; fourth, the relentless drop in price levels (a stark contrast to the inflation of other eras); and finally, the failure of the money supply to keep pace with productivity, a development that drove up interest rates and restricted the availability of credit. (p. 570)

Paragraph 2:

All five factors were closely related. The great bituminous coal deposits in Pennsylvania, West Virginia, and Kentucky provided the cheap energy that fueled the railroads, the factories, and explosive urban growth. Exploiting these inexpensive energy sources, new technologies stimulated productivity and catalyzed the breathtaking industrial expansion. Technology also enabled manufacturers to cut costs and hire cheap unskilled or semi-skilled labor. This cost cutting in turn drove firms to undersell each other, destroying weaker competitors and prompting stronger, more efficient (and more ruthless) ones to consolidate. At least until the mid-1890s, cost reduction, new technology, and fierce competition forced down overall price levels. Farmers and industrial workers suffered from chronically low agricultural commodity prices and wages, but in their capacity as consumers, they (and all Americans) benefitted as store-bought goods cheapened. Meanwhile, high interest rates and the difficulty of obtaining credit added to the burdens of farmers and small entrepreneurs. And almost everyone suffered terribly during the depression years, when the government did nothing to relieve distress. "The sufferings of the working classes are daily increasing," wrote one Philadelphia worker in 1874. "Famine has broken into the home of many of us, and is at the door of all." Above all, business leaders' unflagging drive to maximize efficiency both created colossal fortunes at the top of the economic ladder and forced millions of wage earners to live near the subsistence level. (p. 570)

Paragraph 3:

Out of the new industrial system poured dismal clouds of haze and soot—as well as the first tantalizing trickle of what would become an avalanche of consumer goods. In turn, mounting demands for consumer goods stimulated heavy industry's production of "capital goods"—machines to boost farm and factory output. Together with the railroads, the corporations that manufactured capital goods, refined petroleum, and made steel became the driving force in the nation's economic growth. (p. 570)

Paragraph 4:

A stunning expansion in the *scale* of industry offered tangible evidence of the magnitude of economic change. By the turn of the century, mammoth corporations dominated industrial production. The Singer Sewing Machine Company, for example, with capitalization (operating capital) of $20 million in 1905, boasted eight factories and more than 90,000 employees who made and sold 1.25 million sewing machines annually. Huge companies similarly achieved marvels of production in the railroad, meatpacking, steel, sugar, and oil industries. (pp. 570–571)

Paragraph 5:

Competition among the aggressive and innovative capitalists who headed American heavy industry was intense—and as the post–Civil War era opened, nowhere was it more intense than among the nation's railroads, which to many Americans most symbolized industrial progress. (p. 571)

SUGGESTED RESPONSES for Discussion 9:

Application 9A: The central theme of this passage is stated in the first sentence of the first paragraph: "Five features dominated the birth of modern industrial America after the Civil War. . . ." Every idea in the passage relates to this theme.

Application 9B:

Marginal notes for Paragraph 1:

THE BIRTH OF MODERN INDUSTRIAL AMERICA
(Cause/Effect Pattern)

Five features mark the birth of industrial America after the Civil War.

1. coal as source of cheap energy

2. technology and factory expansion

3. competition (price cutting & consolidation; eliminate rivals/create monopolies

4. drop in price levels

5. failure of money supply to keep pace (higher interest rates & less credit)

Marginal notes for Paragraph 2:

Coal deposits: cheap energy for railroads, factories; contributed to explosive urban growth and new technologies.

Effects of technological changes:
    increased productivity
    industrial expansion
    cost cuts
    use of unskilled, cheap labor
    underselling
    takeovers
    consolidation
    forced prices down
    low prices & wages
    depression
    fortunes for a few
    millions of poor

Marginal notes for Paragraph 3:

Manufacturing:
> many consumer goods
> demand stimulated production of heavy industry
> railroads
> "capital goods"
> increased corporate powers
> machines, oil, steel

Marginal notes for Paragraph 4:

Large Scale Businesses
> dominated production by 1900
> Singer Co., railroad, meatpacking,
> steel, sugar, oil

Marginal notes for Paragraph 5:

Competition intense in heavy industry, especially railroads
railroads: symbolized industrial progress

Compiling Notes for a Complete Passage

Now look at the example below to see how marginal or separate-column notes could work for the complete passage. Read through the notes to see how this system of notetaking might set up a handy review tool. Try paraphrasing and summarizing as you review the notes.

THE CHARACTER OF INDUSTRIAL CHANGE

Five features dominated the birth of modern industrial America after the Civil War: first, the exploitation of immense coal deposits as a source of cheap energy; second, the rapid spread of technological innovation and the factory system; third, the constant pressure on firms to compete tooth and nail by cutting costs and prices, as well as the impulse to eliminate rivals and create monopolies; fourth, the relentless drop in price levels (a stark contrast to the inflation of other eras); and finally, the failure of the money supply to keep pace with productivity, a development that drove up interest rates and restricted the availability of credit.

THE BIRTH OF MODERN
INDUSTRIAL AMERICA
(Cause/Effect Pattern)

Five features mark the birth of industrial America after the Civil War.

1. coal as source of cheap energy
2. technology and factory expansion
3. competition (price cutting & consolidation; eliminate rivals/create monopolies
4. drop in price levels
5. failure of money supply to keep pace. (higher interest & less credit)

All five factors were closely related. The great bituminous coal deposits in Pennsylvania, West Virginia, and Kentucky provided the cheap energy that fueled the railroads, the factories, and explosive urban growth. Exploiting these inexpensive energy sources, new technologies stimulated productivity and catalyzed the breathtaking industrial expansion. Technology also enabled manufacturers to cut costs and hire cheap unskilled or semi-skilled labor. This cost cutting in turn drove firms to undersell each other, destroying weaker competitors and prompting stronger, more efficient (and more ruthless) ones to consolidate. At least until the mid-1890s, cost reduction, new technology, and fierce competition forced down overall price levels. Farmers and industrial workers suffered from chronically low agricultural commodity prices and wages, but in their capacity as consumers, they (and all Americans) benefitted as store-bought goods cheapened. Meanwhile, high interest rates and the difficulty of obtaining credit added to the burdens of farmers and small entrepreneurs. And almost everyone suffered terribly during the depression years, when the government did nothing to relieve distress. "The sufferings of the working classes are daily increasing," wrote one Philadelphia worker in 1874. "Famine has broken into the home of many of us, and is at the door of all." Above all, business leaders' unflagging drive to maximize efficiency both created colossal fortunes at the top of the economic ladder and forced millions of wage earners to live near the subsistence level.

Out of the new industrial system poured dismal clouds of haze and soot—as well as the first tantalizing trickle of what would become an

Coal deposits: cheap energy for railroads, factories; contributed to explosive urban growth and new technologies.

Effects of technological changes:
increased productivity
industrial expansion
cost cuts
use of unskilled, cheap labor
underselling
takeovers
consolidation
forced prices down
low prices & wages
depression
fortunes for a few
millions of poor

Manufacturing:
many consumer goods
demand stimulated production of heavy industry

avalanche of consumer goods. In turn, mounting demands for consumer goods stimulated heavy industry's production of "capital goods"—machines to boost farm and factory output. Together with the railroads, the corporations that manufactured capital goods, refined petroleum, and made steel became the driving force in the nation's economic growth.

> "capital goods"
> railroads
> machines, oil, steel
> increased corporate powers

A stunning expansion in the *scale* of industry offered tangible evidence of the magnitude of economic change. By the turn of the century, mammoth corporations dominated industrial production. The Singer Sewing Machine Company, for example, with capitalization (operating capital) of $20 million in 1905, boasted eight factories and more than 90,000 employees who made and sold 1.25 million sewing machines annually. Huge companies similarly achieved marvels of production in the railroad, meatpacking, steel, sugar, and oil industries.

> Large-scale businesses dominated production by 1900
> Singer Co., railroad, meatpacking steel, sugar, oil

Competition among the aggressive and innovative capitalists who headed American heavy industry was intense— and as the post–Civil War era opened, nowhere was it more intense than among the nation's railroads, which to many Americans most symbolized industrial progress. (p. 570–571)

> Intense competition in heavy industry
> railroads: symbol of industrial progress

DISCUSSION 10: Concept Mapping

Now we come to the most fun, innovative system for study and review: concept mapping. Concept maps provide a "picture" of the ideas, relationships, and details that you are trying to learn. The more complex the ideas, the more interesting and creative mapping them becomes.

The best way to explain a concept map is by example. The maps below were drawn from paragraphs used in Discussion 4, "Reading Paragraphs." Examine each concept map to see how the topic, main idea, and major details can be used to form a picture of essential information.

Example 1:

Tiny though they were, the Dutch and Swedish colonies were historically significant. New Netherland had attained a population of 9,000 and featured a wealthy, thriving port city by the time it came under English rule in 1664. Even short-lived New Sweden left a mark—the log cabin, that durable symbol of the American frontier, which Finnish settlers in the Swedish colony first introduced to the continent. Above all, the two colonies bequeathed an environment characterized by ethnic and religious diversity that would continue in England's "middle colonies." (p. 83)

Map 1:

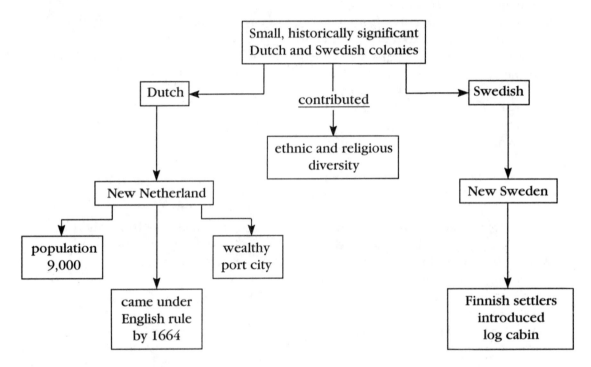

Example 2:

The Americas supplied seemingly limitless wealth for Spain. Not only did some Spaniards grow rich from West Indian sugar plantations and Mexican sheep and cattle ranches, but immense quantities of silver crossed the Atlantic after rich mines in Mexico and Peru began producing in the 1540s. A robust trade between America and Spain grew up, which Castilian officials tried to regulate. Spain took in far more American silver than its economy could absorb, setting off inflation that eventually engulfed all Europe. Bent on dominating Europe, the Spanish kings needed ever more American silver to pay their armies. Several times they went bankrupt, and their efforts to squeeze more taxes from their subjects provoked in the 1560s the revolt of Spain's rich Netherlands provinces—modern Belgium, Holland, and Luxemburg. In the end, gaining access to American wealth cost Spain dearly. (p. 39)

Map 2A:

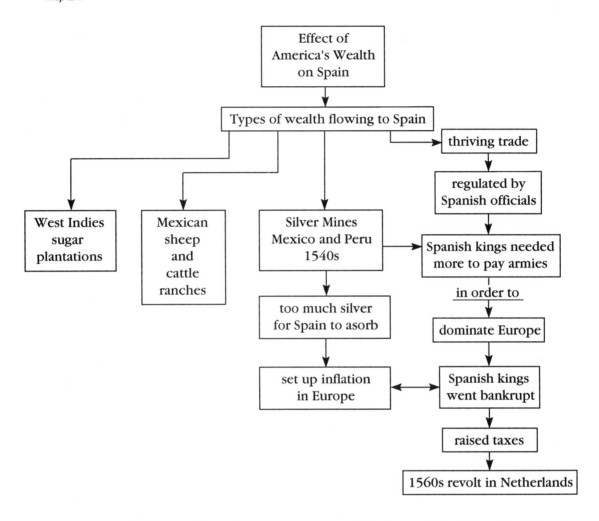

In concept mapping, each reader creates a personalized map. Map 2B on the following page shows another map of the paragraph in Example 2. Compare the two maps. Both work, showing key concepts and relationships. There are other ways that this paragraph could be mapped, and each would be "correct" as long as it showed how key elements in the paragraph related to each other and to the paragraph's main idea.

A concept map may reflect only the barest essentials of ideas and relationships, or it may be quite complex. The example below shows two ways of mapping the following paragraph. Map 3A focuses on the main idea and major details. Map 3B shows a fuller picture of the information presented in the paragraph.

Example:

The War of 1812 had three major political consequences. First, it eliminated the Federalists as a national political force. Second, it went a long way toward convincing the Republicans that the nation was strong and resilient, capable of fighting a war while maintaining the liberty of its people. The third consequence was an outgrowth of the first two. With the Federalists tainted by disloyalty and with fears about the fragility of

Map 2B:

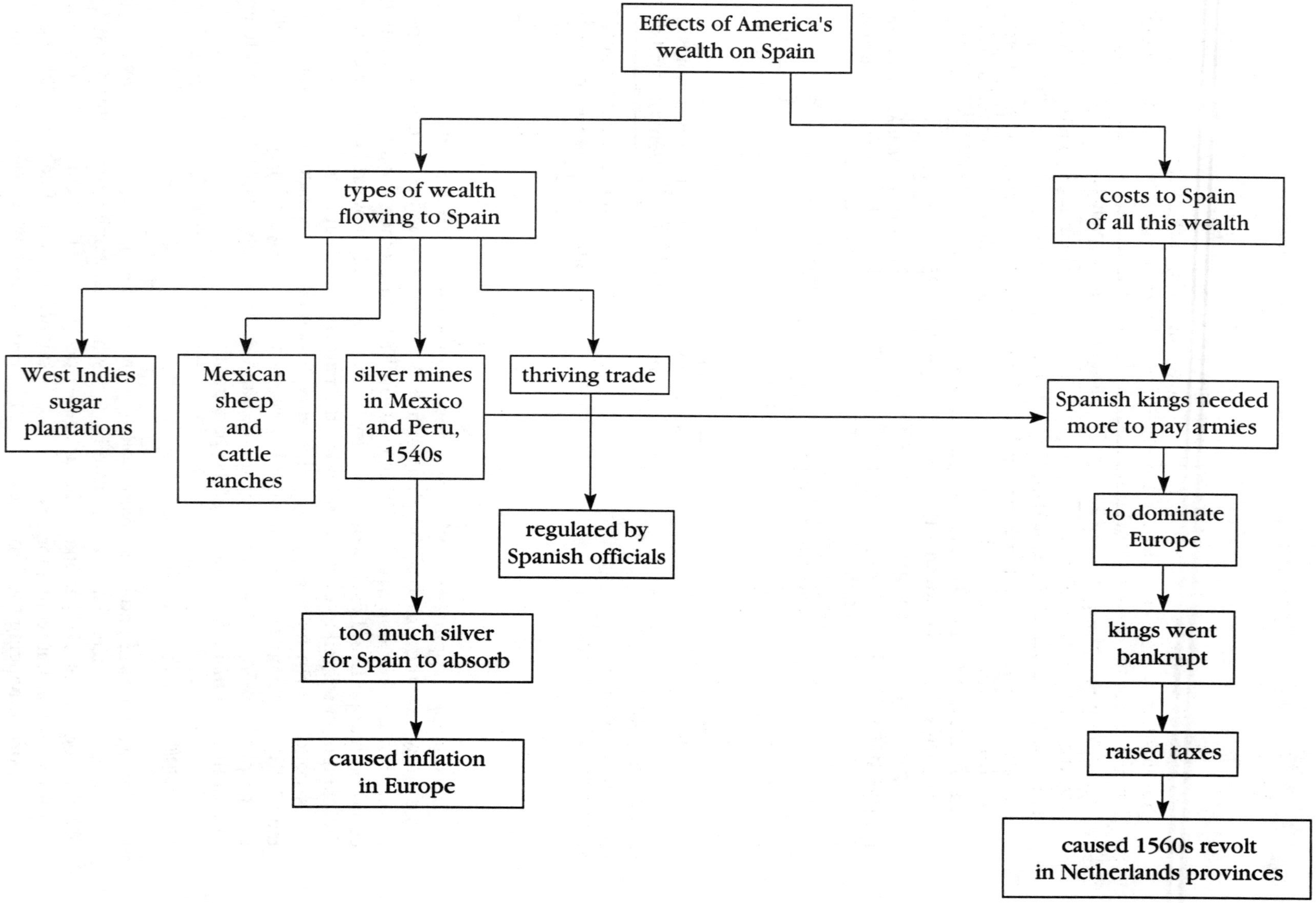

Effects of America's wealth on Spain

costs to Spain of all this wealth → **Spanish kings needed more to pay armies** → **to dominate Europe** → **kings went bankrupt** → **raised taxes** → **caused 1560s revolt in Netherlands provinces**

types of wealth flowing to Spain

- **thriving trade** → **regulated by Spanish officials**
- **silver mines in Mexico and Peru, 1540s** → **too much silver for Spain to absorb** → **caused inflation in Europe**
- **Mexican sheep and cattle ranches**
- **West Indies sugar plantations**

republics fading, Republicans increasingly embraced some doctrines long associated with the Federalists. In a message to Congress in December 1815, Madison called for federal support for internal improvements, tariff protection for the new industries that had sprung up during the embargo, and the creation of a new national bank. (The charter of the first Bank of the United States had expired in 1811.) In Congress another Republican, Henry Clay of Kentucky, proposed similar measures, which he called the American System, with the aim of making the nation economically self-sufficient and free from dependency on Europe. In 1816 Congress chartered the Second Bank of the United States and enacted a moderate tariff. Federal support for internal improvements proved to be a thornier problem. Madison favored federal aid in principle but believed that a constitutional amendment was necessary to authorize it. Accordingly, he vetoed an internal-improvements bill passed in 1817. (pp. 258–259)

Map 3A:

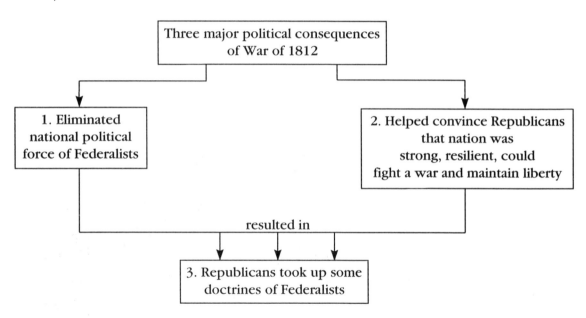

Map 3B:

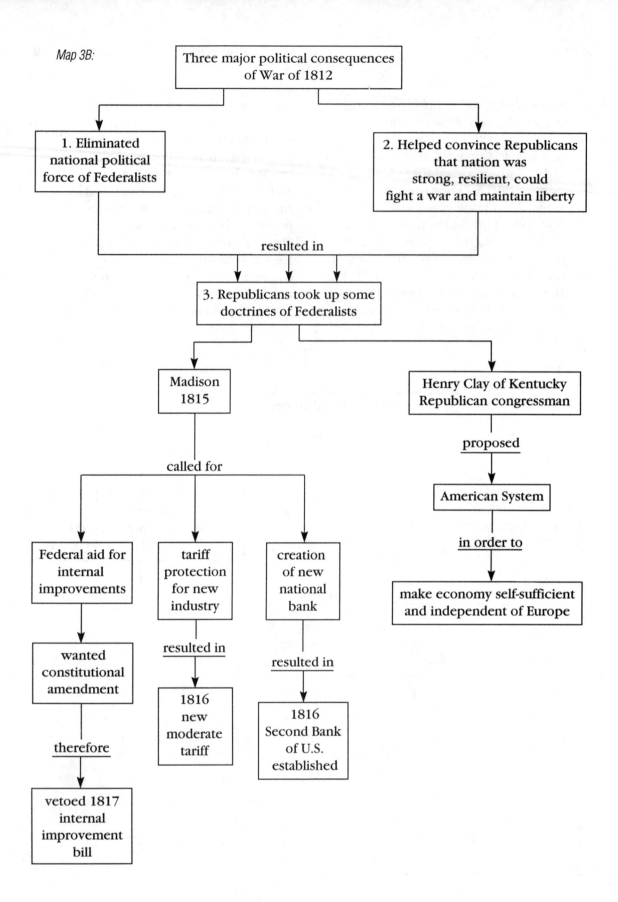

Three major political consequences of War of 1812

1. Eliminated national political force of Federalists

2. Helped convince Republicans that nation was strong, resilient, could fight a war and maintain liberty

resulted in

3. Republicans took up some doctrines of Federalists

Madison 1815

Henry Clay of Kentucky Republican congressman

proposed

American System

in order to

make economy self-sufficient and independent of Europe

called for

Federal aid for internal improvements

tariff protection for new industry

creation of new national bank

wanted constitutional amendment

resulted in

1816 new moderate tariff

resulted in

1816 Second Bank of U.S. established

therefore

vetoed 1817 internal improvement bill

Try building a concept map the next time you review complex reading material. Begin with a simple map and add to it as your understanding of the text deepens. Concept maps are valuable tools for understanding complex ideas and related information and for checking your comprehension of broad concepts. You can create maps to summarize detailed historical events, related events, or entire periods of history. But be careful. Once you've found out how well this system works, you'll be hooked. The great thing about concept mapping is that, by the time you create the picture, you will have learned the material. To review later, all you need to do is re-create the "map." If you can do so, then you *know you know* the information. In fact, the reason that concept mapping works so well is that it forces you to focus on ideas and relationships, so that in the end you understand the broad framework of ideas that is the goal of your study of history. Concept mapping flows naturally from thinking and reading critically.

APPLICATION 10A: Create a concept map for the paragraph shown below. Include as many details as possible. Compare your map with the one in the suggested response.

West African societies changed with the coming of Portuguese slavers. In Guinea and Senegambia, which supplied the bulk of sixteenth-century slaves, small kingdoms expanded to "service" the trade. Some of their rulers became comparatively rich. Farther south, in present-day Angola, the kings of Kongo used the slave trade to consolidate their power and voluntarily adopted Christianity. Kongo flourished until the late sixteenth century, when attackers from the interior destroyed it. (p. 34)

APPLICATION 10B: Create a concept map for the paragraph shown below. Include all major details. Practice showing relationships of details by supplying connecting words that signal the cause/effect pattern by which the details are organized. Compare your map with the one in the suggested response.

The year 1864 proved crucial for the North. While Grant occupied Lee in the East, a Union army under William T. Sherman attacked from Tennessee into northwestern Georgia and took Atlanta in early September. The fall of Atlanta not only boosted northern morale but contributed to Lincoln's reelection. Now the curtain rose on the last act of the war. After taking Atlanta, Sherman marched across Georgia to Savannah, devastated the state's resources, and cracked its morale. Pivoting north from Savannah, Sherman then moved into South Carolina. Meanwhile, having backed Lee into trenches around Petersburg and Richmond, Grant forced the evacuation of both cities and brought on the Confederacy's collapse. (p. 491)

APPLICATION 10C: In Discussion 9, you practiced writing notes for the text passage, "The Character of Industrial Change." Take the opportunity now to create a concept map for the complete passage. Turn to Discussion 9 to review the paragraph and passage notes for "The Character of Industrial Change." Develop a map for each paragraph in the passage; then combine your paragraph concept maps into one large map incorporating all the ideas, details, and relationships that the passage presents. Then see the suggested responses.

SUGGESTED RESPONSES to Discussion 10:

Application 10A:

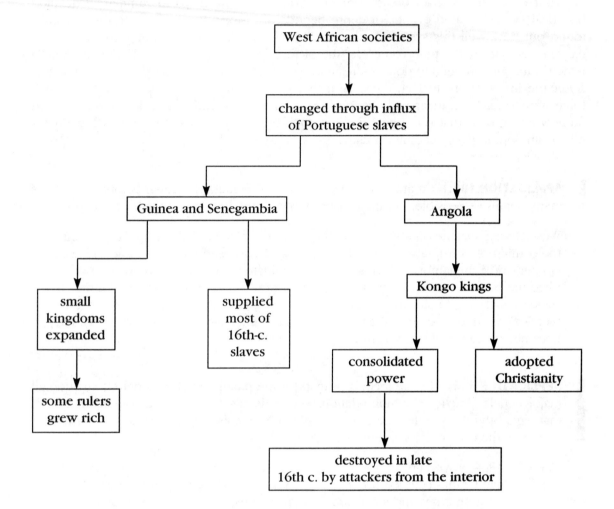

Application 10B:

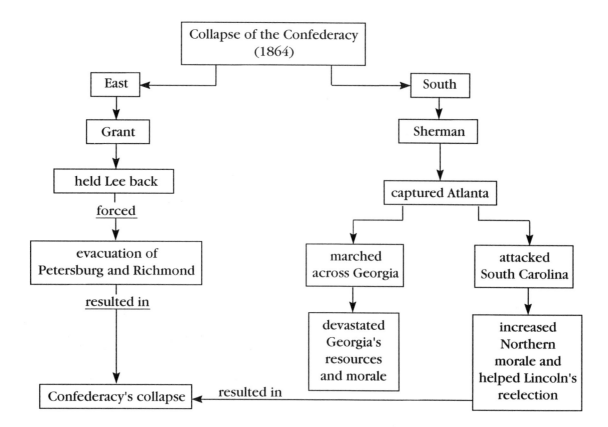

Application 10C:

NOTE: See how the "five dominating features" of post–Civil War American industry shown in Paragraph 1 fit together in the new map on page 97.

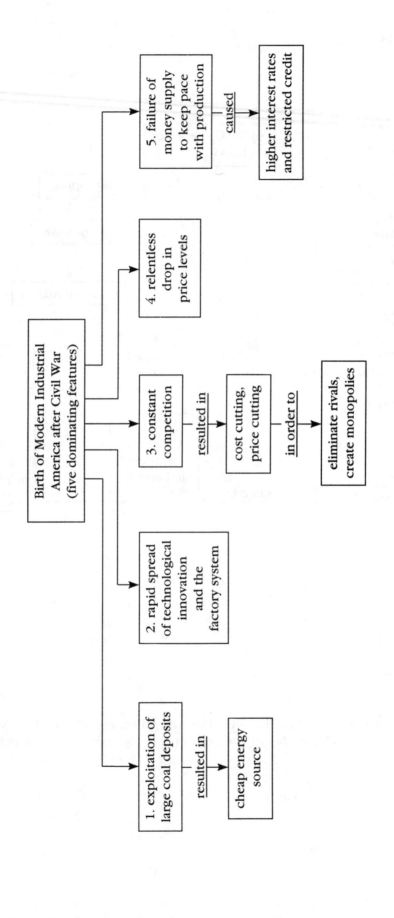

Birth of Modern Industrial America after Civil War (five dominating features)

1. exploitation of large coal deposits — resulted in → cheap energy source

2. rapid spread of technological innovation and the factory system

3. constant competition — resulted in → cost cutting, price cutting — in order to → eliminate rivals, create monopolies

4. relentless drop in price levels

5. failure of money supply to keep pace with production — caused → higher interest rates and restricted credit

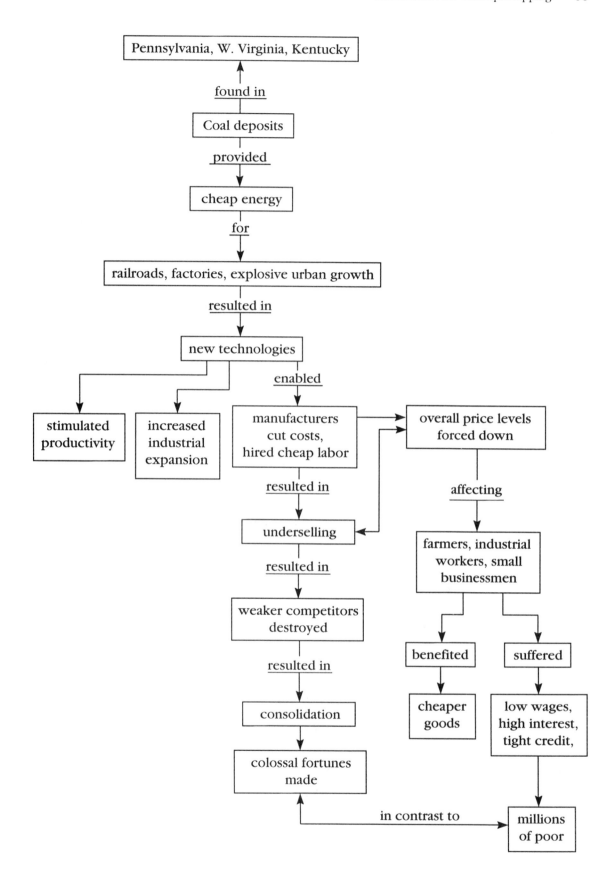

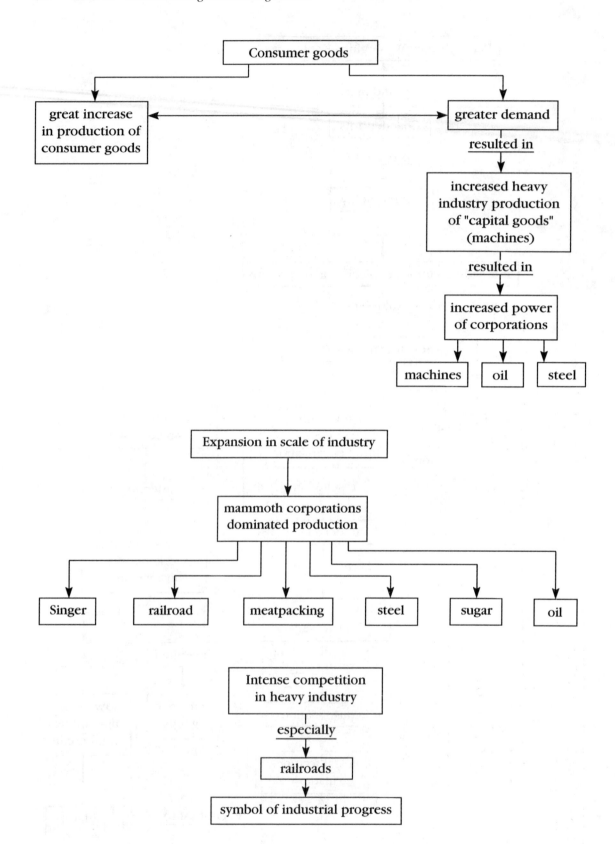

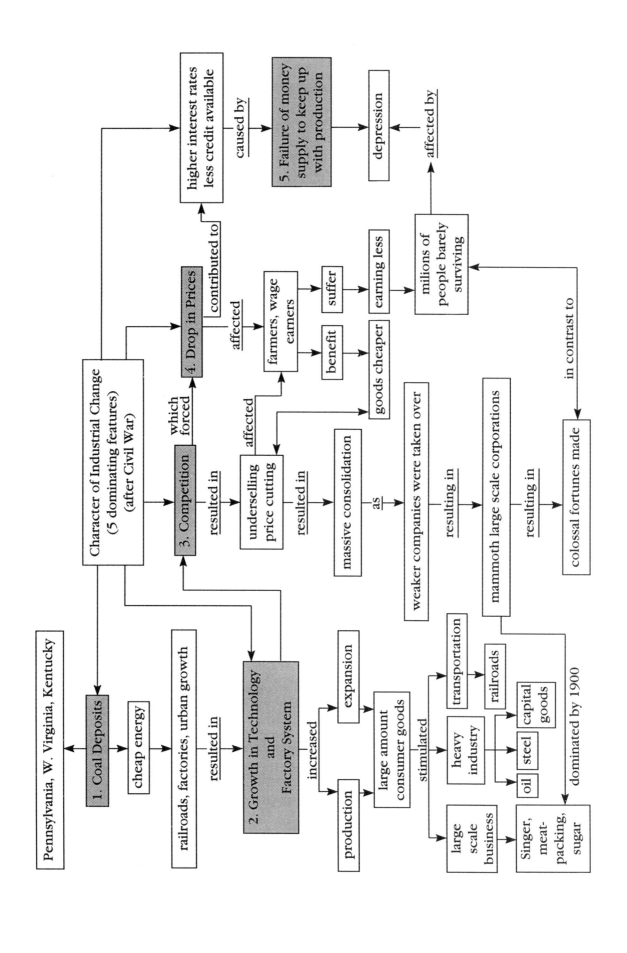

CONGRATULATIONS!

Congratulations on finishing *Critical Reading*! By now you've gained some familiarity with the historian's craft. You've begun thinking like a historian, and you know how to get *and retain* the information you need from your textbook. Experiment with the various reading, reviewing, and note-taking techniques that you've learned here; try them when studying for your next exam, whether in your history course or another course. By using even just a few of these new tools, you'll be on your way to *reading and thinking critically*.

BIBLIOGRAPHY

Boyer, Paul S., et al. *The Enduring Vision: A History of The American People*. 2nd ed. Lexington: D. C. Heath, 1993.

Bradford, William. *Of Plymoth Plantation 1620–1647*. Ed. Samuel E. Morison. New York: Random House, 1952.

Brown, Neil M., and Stuart M. Keeley. *Asking the Right Questions: A Guide to Critical Thinking*. 3rd ed. New Jersey: Prentice Hall, 1990.

Chaffee, John. *Thinking Critically*. 3rd ed. Boston: Houghton Mifflin, 1990.

"Excerpts from Statements by U.S. and Iraq Feb. 22–Feb. 28." *Facts on File* Feb. 1991: 133–135.

Davidson, James West. *Nations of Nations: A Narrative History of the American Republic*. 2nd ed. McGraw-Hill, 1994.

Grant, Robert B., and James J. Lorence. *Instructor's Guide to Accompany The Enduring Vision*. Lexington: D. C. Heath, 1993.

Jennings, Francis. *The Invasion of America*. Chapel Hill: University of North Carolina Press, 1975.

Lawson, John. "Customs of the Noble Savage." *This Country Was Ours*. Virgil Vogil. New York: Harper & Row, 1972. 43–44.

Norton, Mary Beth, et al. *A People and a Nation: A History of the United States*. 4th ed. Boston: Houghton Mifflin, 1994.

Paul, Richard. *Critical Thinking*. Rohnert Park: Sonoma State University, 1990.

Proceedings of the Twelfth Annual International Conference on Critical Thinking and Educational Reform. Conference Theme. By Cynthia Barnes et al. Rohnert Park: Sonoma State University, 1992.

Record, Jeffrey. *Hollow Victory, A Contrary View of the Gulf War*. Washington: Brassey's (US), 1993.

Rowlandson, Mary. "A Narrative of the Captivity and Restoration of Mrs. Mary Rowlandson." *The Heath Anthology of American Literature*.

Rowlandson, Mary. "A Narrative of the Captivity and Restauration of Mrs. Mary Rowlandson." *The Heath Anthology of American Literature*. Vol. 1, 2nd ed. Lexington: D. C. Heath, 1994, 343–366.

Stout, Neil R. *Getting the Most out of Your U.S. History Course, The History Student's Vade Mecum*. Lexington: D. C. Heath, 1993.